Essential Maths 8C

Homework Book

Elmwood Press

First published 2009 by
Elmwood Press
80 Attimore Road
Welwyn Garden City
Herts. Al8 6LP
Tel. 01707 333232

Reprinted 2012

ISBN 9781 906 622 138

Typeset and illustrated by Domex e-Data Pvt. Ltd.
Printed and bound by Bookwell

CONTENTS

Unit 1   **Page**

1.1 Sequences   1
1.2 Fractions   2
1.3 Properties of numbers   6
1.4 Negative numbers   9
1.5 Area and Perimeter   12

Unit 2

2.1 Rounding off and estimating   18
2.2 Using Algebra   20
2.3 Fractions, decimals, percentages   23
2.4 Geometrical Reasoning   25
2.5 Construction and Locus   28
2.6 Circles   31

Unit 3

3.1 Written Calculations   35
3.2 Using a calculator   40
3.3 Formulas and expressions   44
3.4 Drawing graphs   47
3.5 Reflection   53

Unit 4

4.1 Describing data   57
4.2 Rotation and combined transformations   61
4.3 Interpreting and sketching real-life graphs   64
4.4 Brackets and equations   66
4.5 Fractions review   72
4.6 Handling data   75

Unit 5

5.1 Ratio and proportion   80
5.2 Negative numbers review   83
5.3 Sequences – the nth term   84
5.4 Enlargement   89
5.5 Congruent shapes, tessellation   93
5.6 Drawing graphs review   94
5.7 Area review   96

Unit 6

6.1 Percentages   98
6.2 Probability   102
6.3 Measures   106
6.4 Algebra review   108
6.5 3–D Objects   111
6.6 Bearings and scale drawing   112
6.7 Decimals review   116
6.8 Volume   117

UNIT 1

1.1 Sequences

| Main Book Page 1

1 The first term of a sequence is 29. Write down the first six terms of the sequence if the rule is:

(a) add 7   (b) subtract 10   (c) multiply by 10

2 Write down the rule for each sequence.

(a) 3.3, 3.1, 2.9, 2.7, ...   (b) 3.5, 7, 14, 28, ...

(c) 60, 6, 0.6, 0.06, ...   (d) −7, −5, −3, −1, ...

3 Write down each sequence and find the missing numbers.

(a) | 3 | 12 | 48 | | |

(b) | −4 | −1 | | 5 | 8 | |

(c) | | | | 11 | 6 | 1 |

4 (a)

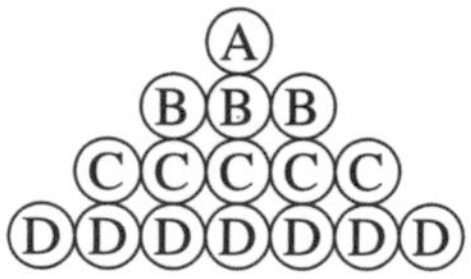

     (A)
   (B)(B)(B)
  (C)(C)(C)(C)
(D)(D)(D)(D)(D)(D)

Draw the next row which will fit onto the bottom of this triangle.

(b) How many circles are used in total for the triangle in part (a) if seven rows are drawn?

5 Luke says the next number in the sequence | 1 | 2 | 4 | is | 8 | . Ali says that he is wrong and the next number is | 7 | . Tom says that they are both correct. *Explain* why.

HWK 1E ──────────────────────────────── **Main Book Page 2**

1 The first term of a sequence is 4. Write down the first four terms of the sequence if the rule is:

(a) double and subtract 1

(b) multiply by 3 and add 1

(c) double and add 4

2 Find the missing numbers in these linear sequences.

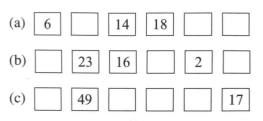

(a) | 6 | | 14 | 18 | | |

(b) | | 23 | 16 | | 2 | |

(c) | | 49 | | | | 17 |

3 A linear sequence has a 3rd term of 15 and a 4th term of 19. What is the 2nd term?

4 A linear sequence has a 1st term of 7 and a 3rd term of 19. What is the 4th term?

5 The rule for this sequence is 'multiply by 2 and add 2'. Find the missing numbers.

6 Write down the rule for this sequence.

1.2 Fractions

HWK 1M ──────────────────────────────── **Main Book Page 5**

1 Write the shaded areas as both mixed numbers and improper fractions.

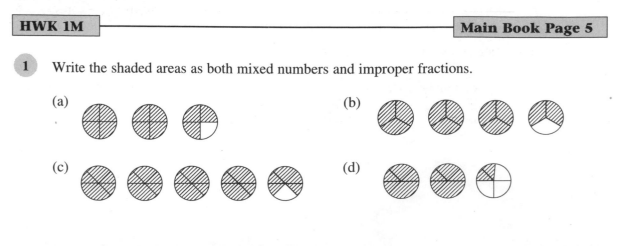

(a)

(b)

(c)

(d)

2 Change these improper fractions to mixed numbers or whole numbers only.

(a) $\frac{7}{2}$ (b) $\frac{13}{3}$ (c) $\frac{14}{5}$ (d) $\frac{13}{4}$ (e) $\frac{23}{7}$

(f) $\frac{11}{6}$ (g) $\frac{33}{10}$ (h) $\frac{21}{8}$ (i) $\frac{15}{7}$ (j) $\frac{29}{5}$

HWK 1E ———————————————————— **Main Book Page 5**

1 Change the mixed numbers to improper fractions.

(a) $4\frac{2}{3}$ (b) $2\frac{1}{4}$ (c) $5\frac{3}{4}$ (d) $7\frac{1}{2}$ (e) $3\frac{4}{5}$

(f) $5\frac{3}{8}$ (g) $2\frac{7}{9}$ (h) $6\frac{1}{6}$ (i) $4\frac{2}{5}$ (j) $5\frac{7}{10}$

2 Match up the improper fractions to the mixed numbers (beware: there is one odd one out).

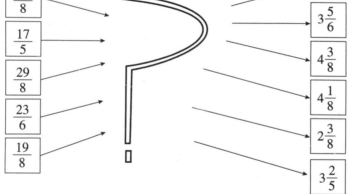

HWK 2M ———————————————————— **Main Book Page 6**

1 Which fraction is *not* equivalent to the others?

2 Copy and complete

(a) $\frac{3}{4} - \frac{1}{8}$

$= \frac{\square}{8} - \frac{1}{8}$

$= \frac{\square}{8}$

(b) $\frac{1}{3} + \frac{2}{15}$

$= \frac{\square}{15} + \frac{2}{15}$

$= \frac{\square}{15}$

(c) $\frac{11}{20} - \frac{1}{4}$

$= \frac{11}{20} - \frac{\square}{20}$

$= \frac{\square}{20} = \frac{\square}{10}$

3 Work out

(a) $\frac{1}{8} + \frac{3}{16}$

(b) $\frac{9}{20} - \frac{1}{4}$

(c) $\frac{11}{30} - \frac{1}{6}$

(d) $\frac{1}{12} + \frac{2}{3}$

(e) $\frac{5}{21} - \frac{1}{7}$

(f) $\frac{23}{40} - \frac{2}{5}$

4 Ben carpets $\frac{5}{8}$ of his new house. He uses wood flooring for $\frac{1}{4}$ of the house. The remaining floor area in his house is tiled. What fraction of the floor area is tiled?

5 Answer true or false:

(a) $\frac{18}{24} = \frac{3}{4}$

(b) $\frac{7}{8} = \frac{24}{32}$

(c) $\frac{5}{9} = \frac{20}{36}$

(d) $\frac{24}{28} = \frac{6}{7}$

(e) $\frac{30}{42} = \frac{4}{7}$

(f) $\frac{3}{10} = \frac{21}{70}$

HWK 2E ———————————————————————— **Main Book Page 8**

1 Work out

(a) $\frac{3}{5} - \frac{1}{3}$

(b) $\frac{1}{4} + \frac{2}{3}$

(c) $\frac{2}{5} + \frac{3}{8}$

(d) $\frac{5}{7} - \frac{1}{8}$

(e) $\frac{1}{2} - \frac{3}{7}$

(f) $\frac{2}{9} + \frac{3}{10}$

(g) $\frac{7}{8} - \frac{2}{3}$

(h) $\frac{9}{10} - \frac{5}{7}$

2 Louise and Jake are sharing a pizza. Louise eats $\frac{2}{5}$ of the pizza and Jake eats $\frac{3}{7}$ of the pizza. What fraction of the pizza is left?

3 Work out, leaving each answer as a mixed number.

(a) $1\frac{1}{4} + 1\frac{1}{3}$

(b) $3\frac{1}{3} + 2\frac{1}{3}$

(c) $4\frac{3}{4} - 3\frac{1}{3}$

(d) $2\frac{1}{3} - \frac{5}{8}$

(e) $1\frac{1}{3} + 2\frac{5}{6}$

(f) $4\frac{1}{2} - 2\frac{7}{8}$

4 A test has 4 parts. This chart shows what fraction of the test each part is.

Part A	Part B	Part C	Part D
$\frac{1}{3}$	$\frac{1}{5}$	$\frac{1}{4}$	?

(a) What fraction of the test is part D?

(b) Janice has completed parts A and B. What fraction of the test has she still got to do?

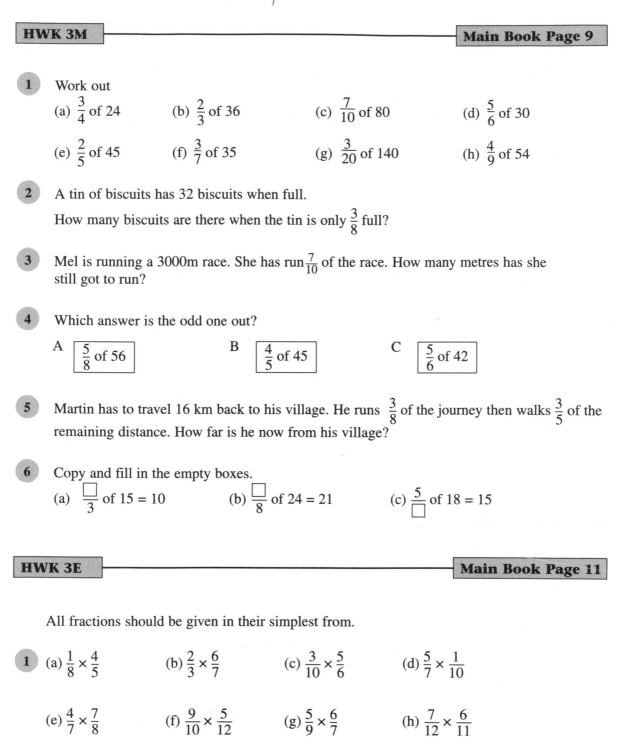

1 Work out

(a) $\frac{3}{4}$ of 24   (b) $\frac{2}{3}$ of 36   (c) $\frac{7}{10}$ of 80   (d) $\frac{5}{6}$ of 30

(e) $\frac{2}{5}$ of 45   (f) $\frac{3}{7}$ of 35   (g) $\frac{3}{20}$ of 140   (h) $\frac{4}{9}$ of 54

2 A tin of biscuits has 32 biscuits when full.

How many biscuits are there when the tin is only $\frac{3}{8}$ full?

3 Mel is running a 3000m race. She has run $\frac{7}{10}$ of the race. How many metres has she still got to run?

4 Which answer is the odd one out?

A $\boxed{\frac{5}{8} \text{ of } 56}$ B $\boxed{\frac{4}{5} \text{ of } 45}$ C $\boxed{\frac{5}{6} \text{ of } 42}$

5 Martin has to travel 16 km back to his village. He runs $\frac{3}{8}$ of the journey then walks $\frac{3}{5}$ of the remaining distance. How far is he now from his village?

6 Copy and fill in the empty boxes.

(a) $\frac{\square}{3}$ of 15 = 10   (b) $\frac{\square}{8}$ of 24 = 21   (c) $\frac{5}{\square}$ of 18 = 15

All fractions should be given in their simplest from.

1 (a) $\frac{1}{8} \times \frac{4}{5}$ (b) $\frac{2}{3} \times \frac{6}{7}$ (c) $\frac{3}{10} \times \frac{5}{6}$ (d) $\frac{5}{7} \times \frac{1}{10}$

(e) $\frac{4}{7} \times \frac{7}{8}$ (f) $\frac{9}{10} \times \frac{5}{12}$ (g) $\frac{5}{9} \times \frac{6}{7}$ (h) $\frac{7}{12} \times \frac{6}{11}$

6

2

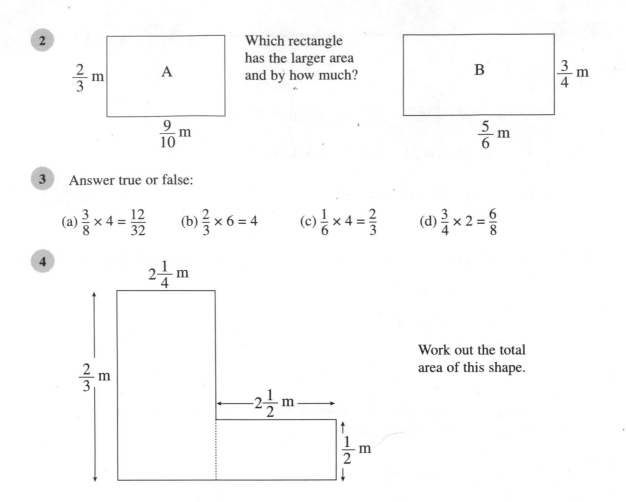

$\frac{2}{3}$ m | A | $\frac{9}{10}$ m

Which rectangle has the larger area and by how much?

B | $\frac{3}{4}$ m | $\frac{5}{6}$ m

3 Answer true or false:

(a) $\frac{3}{8} \times 4 = \frac{12}{32}$ (b) $\frac{2}{3} \times 6 = 4$ (c) $\frac{1}{6} \times 4 = \frac{2}{3}$ (d) $\frac{3}{4} \times 2 = \frac{6}{8}$

4

$2\frac{1}{4}$ m

$\frac{2}{3}$ m

$2\frac{1}{2}$ m

$\frac{1}{2}$ m

Work out the total area of this shape.

1.3 Properties of numbers

HWK 1M ──────────────────────── **Main Book Page 13**

1 Which number below is *not* a factor of 40?

| 20 | | 8 | | 4 | | 5 | | 6 | | 10 |

2 Write down all the prime numbers between 10 and 20.

3 Which numbers below are multiples of 7?

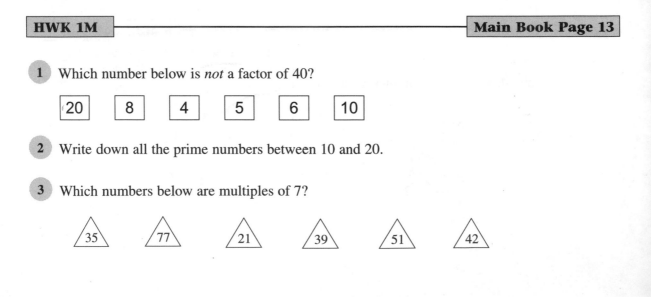

△ 35   △ 77   △ 21   △ 39   △ 51   △ 42

4 'The sum of all the prime numbers less than 8 is 17'. True or false?

5 Work out $6^2 + 4^2 - 5^2$

6 Write down two prime numbers which add up to 28?

7 Write down all the factors of 32.

8 Three factors of 20 add up to 16. Write down two different ways in which this can be done.

| **HWK 1E** | **Main Book Page 14** |

1 (a) List all the factors of 30.

(b) List all the factors of 48.

(c) Write down the highest common factor of 30 and 48.

2 Copy and fill in the empty boxes for this sequence.

| 1 | 3 | 6 | 10 | ⁵ | 21 | ⁷ | ⁸ | 45 |

3 (a) Write down the first six multiples of 15.

(b) Write down the first six multiples of 20.

(c) Write down the lowest common multiple of 15 and 20.

4

True story?
A dog had to have 13 golf balls removed from his stomach after eating them during walks. Oscar, a black labrador, was taken to the vet after his owner noticed a rattling noise coming from his pet's stomach. The dog needed no stitches after the operation and is now said to be in good health!

If the dog had eaten the next highest prime number worth of golf balls, how many golf balls would have been removed from his stomach?

8

5 Find the lowest common multiple of 18 and 30.

6 Find the highest common factor of 28 and 63.

7 Why can a prime number *not* have 0 as its last digit?

8 A baker's van delivers to a village every 5 days. A butcher's van delivers every 7 days. How often will the baker and butcher deliver on the same day?

HWK 2M ────────────────────────────── **Main Book Page 16**

1 Copy and complete this factor tree.

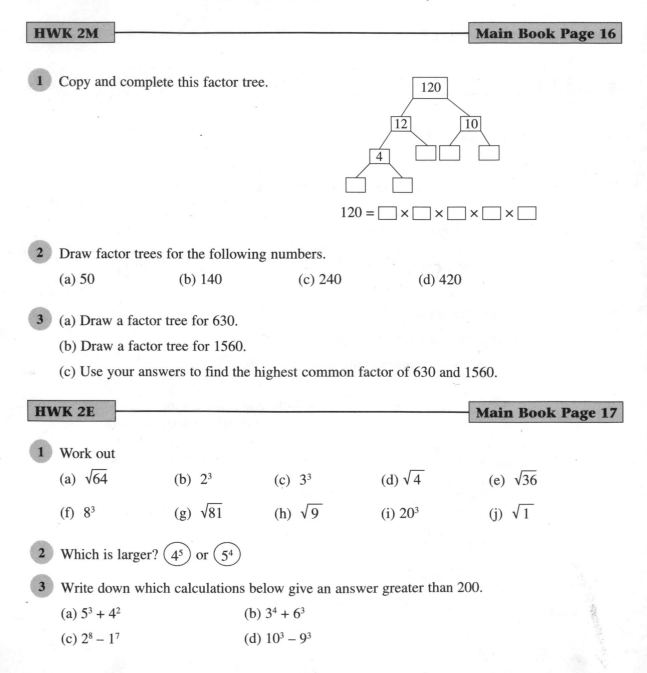

$$120 = \square \times \square \times \square \times \square \times \square$$

2 Draw factor trees for the following numbers.

(a) 50   (b) 140   (c) 240   (d) 420

3 (a) Draw a factor tree for 630.

(b) Draw a factor tree for 1560.

(c) Use your answers to find the highest common factor of 630 and 1560.

HWK 2E ────────────────────────────── **Main Book Page 17**

1 Work out

(a) $\sqrt{64}$ (b) 2^3 (c) 3^3 (d) $\sqrt{4}$ (e) $\sqrt{36}$

(f) 8^3 (g) $\sqrt{81}$ (h) $\sqrt{9}$ (i) 20^3 (j) $\sqrt{1}$

2 Which is larger? 4^5 or 5^4

3 Write down which calculations below give an answer greater than 200.

(a) $5^3 + 4^2$ (b) $3^4 + 6^3$

(c) $2^8 - 1^7$ (d) $10^3 - 9^3$

4 Estimate which is larger? $\boxed{2^6}$ or $\boxed{60 + \sqrt{10}}$

5 '5 to the power of 5 is 3125'. True or false?

6 Work out, without a calculator.

(a) 12^2 　　　(b) $\left(\frac{1}{4}\right)^2$ 　　　(c) 10^4 　　　(d) 0.4^2 　　　(e) 0.1^3

1.4 Negative numbers

| HWK 1M | Main Book Page 20 |

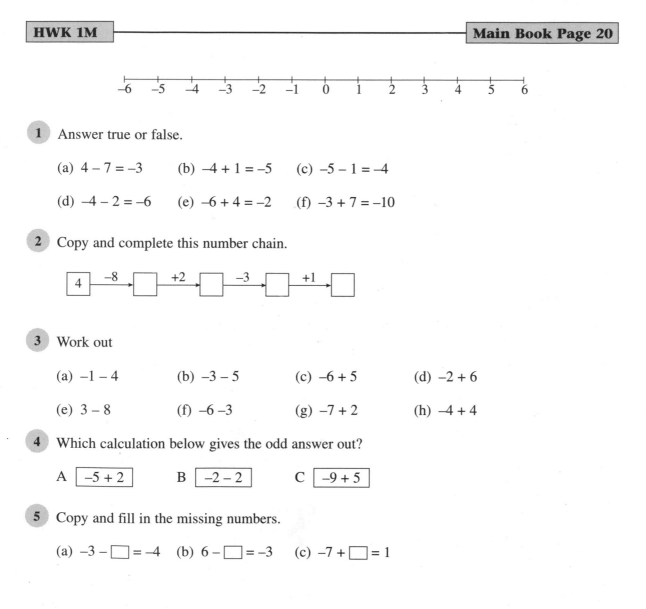

1 Answer true or false.

(a) $4 - 7 = -3$ 　　　(b) $-4 + 1 = -5$ 　　　(c) $-5 - 1 = -4$

(d) $-4 - 2 = -6$ 　　　(e) $-6 + 4 = -2$ 　　　(f) $-3 + 7 = -10$

2 Copy and complete this number chain.

3 Work out

(a) $-1 - 4$ 　　　(b) $-3 - 5$ 　　　(c) $-6 + 5$ 　　　(d) $-2 + 6$

(e) $3 - 8$ 　　　(f) $-6 - 3$ 　　　(g) $-7 + 2$ 　　　(h) $-4 + 4$

4 Which calculation below gives the odd answer out?

A $\boxed{-5 + 2}$ 　　　B $\boxed{-2 - 2}$ 　　　C $\boxed{-9 + 5}$

5 Copy and fill in the missing numbers.

(a) $-3 - \square = -4$ 　　(b) $6 - \square = -3$ 　　(c) $-7 + \square = 1$

6 Jacob has four cards as shown below.

$$\boxed{-6} \quad \boxed{-2} \quad \boxed{3} \quad \boxed{1}$$

He needs to choose one more card which will make the total of all 5 cards equal to –5. Draw the card he needs.

HWK 1E ———————————————————— **Main Book Page 21**

1 Answer true or false.

(a) $7 + (-3) = 4$ (b) $3 - (-1) = 2$ (c) $7 - (-2) = 5$

(d) $3 - (+2) = 5$ (e) $7 + (-5) = 2$ (f) $5 - (-3) = 8$

2 Copy and complete this number chain.

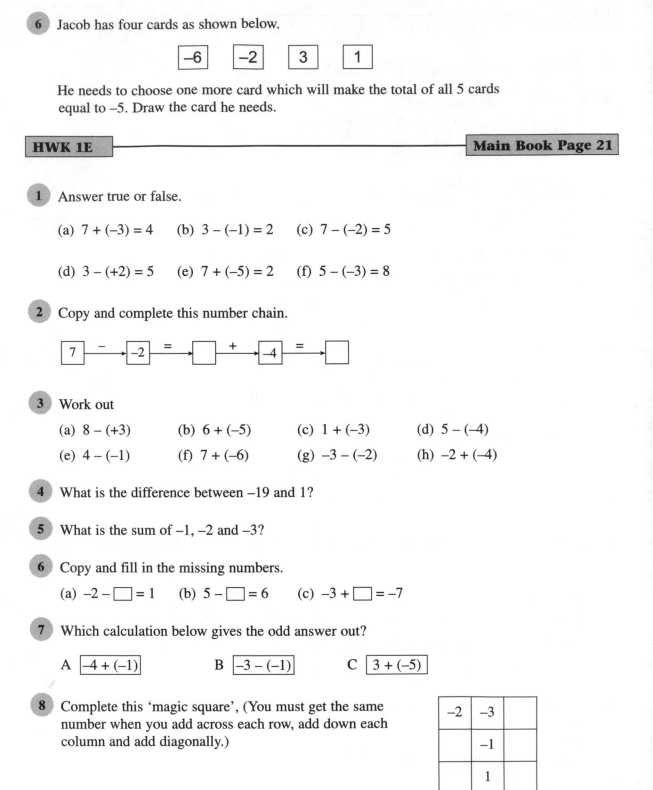

3 Work out

(a) $8 - (+3)$ (b) $6 + (-5)$ (c) $1 + (-3)$ (d) $5 - (-4)$

(e) $4 - (-1)$ (f) $7 + (-6)$ (g) $-3 - (-2)$ (h) $-2 + (-4)$

4 What is the difference between –19 and 1?

5 What is the sum of –1, –2 and –3?

6 Copy and fill in the missing numbers.

(a) $-2 - \square = 1$ (b) $5 - \square = 6$ (c) $-3 + \square = -7$

7 Which calculation below gives the odd answer out?

A $\boxed{-4 + (-1)}$ B $\boxed{-3 - (-1)}$ C $\boxed{3 + (-5)}$

8 Complete this 'magic square', (You must get the same number when you add across each row, add down each column and add diagonally.)

-2	-3	
	-1	
	1	

HWK 2M ────────────────────────────── **Main Book Page 23**

1 Work out

(a) $4 \times (-3)$ (b) $-2 \times (-6)$ (c) $-8 \times (-3)$ (d) -7×2

(e) $-5 \times (-2)$ (f) $2 \times (-9)$ (g) $6 \times (-6)$ (h) $-4 \times (-1)$

(i) $-7 \times (-6)$ (j) $-3 \times (-9)$ (k) $10 \times (-4)$ (l) -20×3

2 The temperature in Glasgow is –4°C. The temperature in Toronto is six times as cold. What is the temperature in Toronto?

3 Which question below gives the highest answer and by how much?

$-4 \times (-4)$ $5 \times (-4)$

4 Copy and complete this number chain.

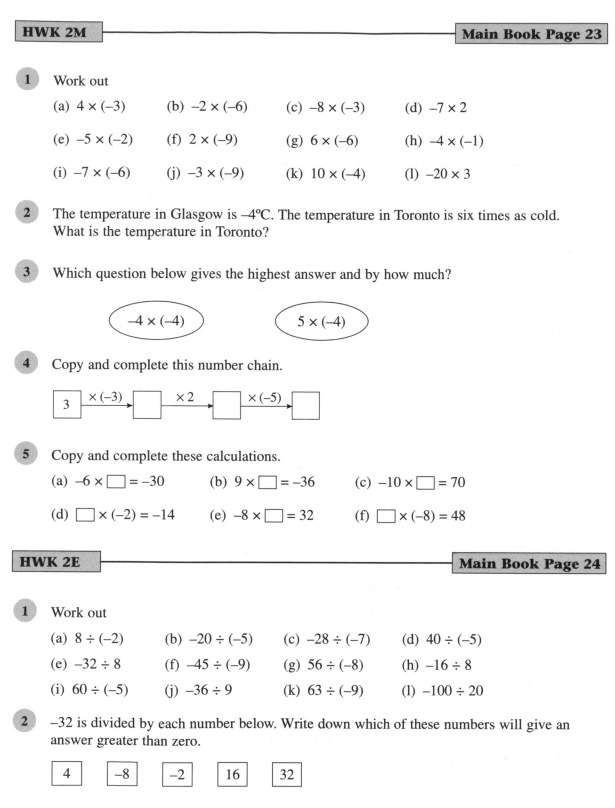

$$3 \xrightarrow{\times (-3)} \square \xrightarrow{\times 2} \square \xrightarrow{\times (-5)} \square$$

5 Copy and complete these calculations.

(a) $-6 \times \square = -30$ (b) $9 \times \square = -36$ (c) $-10 \times \square = 70$

(d) $\square \times (-2) = -14$ (e) $-8 \times \square = 32$ (f) $\square \times (-8) = 48$

HWK 2E ────────────────────────────── **Main Book Page 24**

1 Work out

(a) $8 \div (-2)$ (b) $-20 \div (-5)$ (c) $-28 \div (-7)$ (d) $40 \div (-5)$

(e) $-32 \div 8$ (f) $-45 \div (-9)$ (g) $56 \div (-8)$ (h) $-16 \div 8$

(i) $60 \div (-5)$ (j) $-36 \div 9$ (k) $63 \div (-9)$ (l) $-100 \div 20$

2 –32 is divided by each number below. Write down which of these numbers will give an answer greater than zero.

| 4 | –8 | –2 | 16 | 32 |

3 Answer true or false.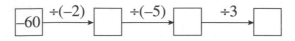

(a) $-3 \times (-3) = -9$

(b) $(-3)^2 = 9$

(c) $-5 \times (-4) = 20$

(d) $2 \times (-3) \times (-4) = 24$

(e) $(-5)^2 = 10$

(f) $-1 \times (-1) \times (-1) = -1$

4 Copy and complete this number chain.

$$-60 \xrightarrow{\div(-2)} \square \xrightarrow{\div(-5)} \square \xrightarrow{\div 3} \square$$

5 Copy and complete this multiplication table.

$\times$	-5		
		-9	6
4			-8
	35		

1.5 Area and Perimeter

HWK 1M   **Main Book Page 28**

1 Calculate the area of each shape. The lengths are in cm.

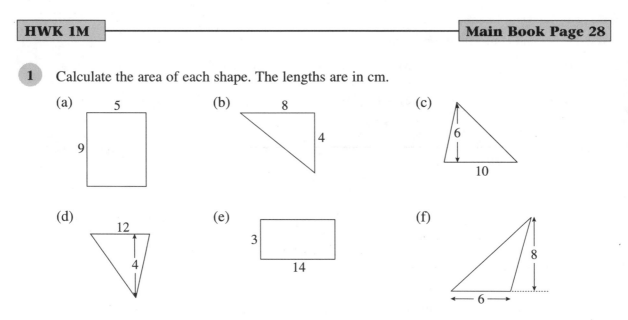

(a)
5
9

(b)
8
4

(c)
6
10

(d)
12
4

(e)
3
14

(f)
8
6

2

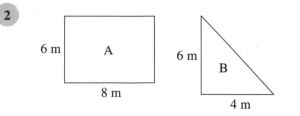

(a) Find the area of shape A.

(b) Find the area of shape B.

(c) Find the total area of both shape A and shape B.

(d) Find the area of this shape.

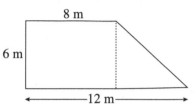

3 Calculate the area of each shape. The lengths are in cm.

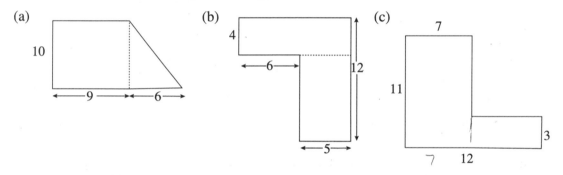

(a)

(b)

(c)

4

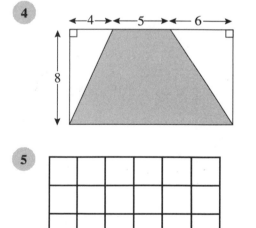

Calculate the shaded area. (all lengths are in cm)

5

Rearrange these 1 cm squares and draw two different rectangles using all the squares. Write down the perimeter of each of your rectangles.

14

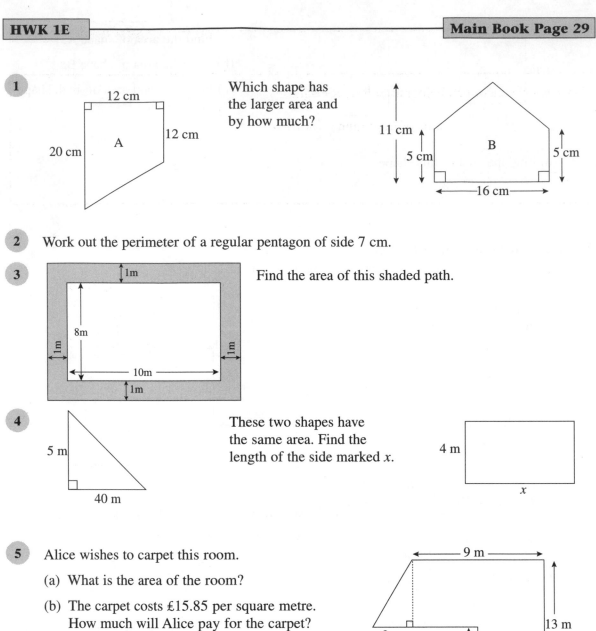

1 Which shape has the larger area and by how much?

12 cm

12 cm

20 cm

A

11 cm

5 cm

B

5 cm

16 cm

2 Work out the perimeter of a regular pentagon of side 7 cm.

3 Find the area of this shaded path.

1m

8m

1m

1m

10m

1m

4 These two shapes have the same area. Find the length of the side marked x.

5 m

40 m

4 m

x

5 Alice wishes to carpet this room.

(a) What is the area of the room?

(b) The carpet costs £15.85 per square metre. How much will Alice pay for the carpet?

9 m

2 m

13 m

5 m

4 m

> *Remember:* area of parallelogram = base × height
>
> area of trapezium = $\frac{1}{2}h(a + b)$

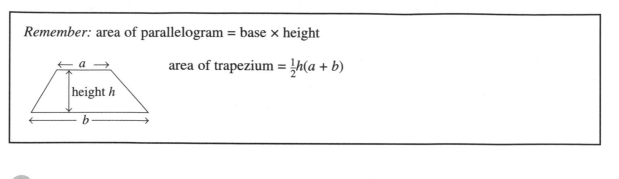

1 Calculate the area of each shape. The lengths are in cm.

(a)   5, 10, 8

(b)   14, 12, 6

(c)   10, 17

(d)   9, 13

(e)   11, 20, 5

(f)   7, 16, 23

2 Calculate the value of x in each parallelogram below.

(a)   area = 84 m^2 x —12 m—

(b)   area = 135 m^2 15 m x

3

Which shape has the larger area and by how much?

shape A — 16 cm, 12 cm, 9 cm

shape B — 10 cm, 14.5 cm

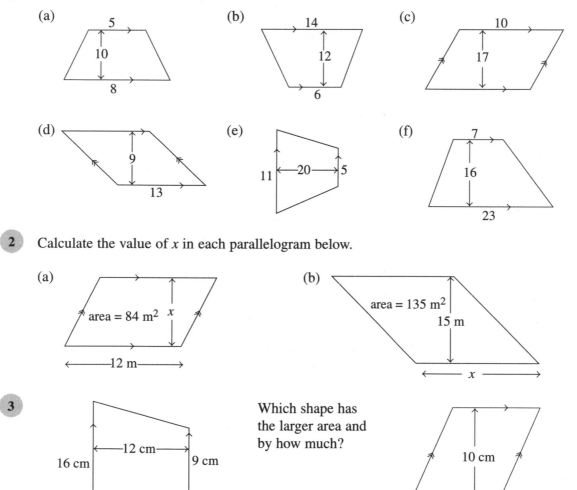

16

1   Jed is putting tiles onto a rectangular wall which measures 3 m by 5 m. Each tile is a square with side 10 cm. A box of 25 tiles costs £9.85.

(a) How many tiles does Jed need?

(b) How much will Jed have to pay for the tiles?

(c) Jed ends up breaking 5% of the tiles. How much *extra* must he spend on the tiles to finish the job?

2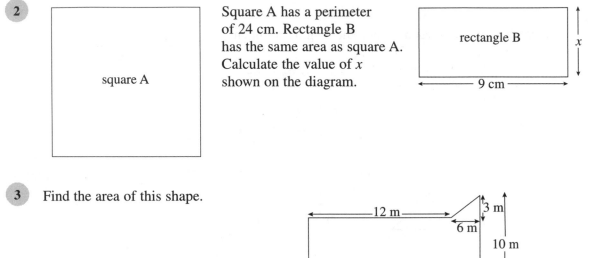

square A

Square A has a perimeter of 24 cm. Rectangle B has the same area as square A. Calculate the value of x shown on the diagram.

rectangle B

x

9 cm

3   Find the area of this shape.

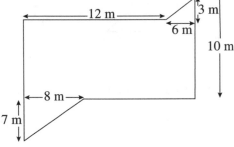

12 m

3 m

6 m

10 m

8 m

7 m

4   area = 54 cm^2

The length of this rectangle is 3 cm greater than its width.
Find the perimeter of this rectangle.

5

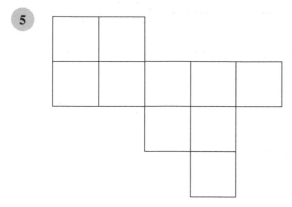

This shape has an area
of 160 cm².
Find the perimeter of this shape.

6 Ashley has to paint one side of his house.
Each pot of paint covers 20 m².
How many pots of paint will Ashley
need to buy to do the job?

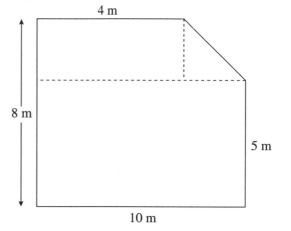

UNIT 2

2.1 Rounding off and estimating

HWK 1M ──────────────────────────────── **Main Book Page 44**

1 Round off these numbers to one decimal place.

(a) 8.69   (b) 6.46   (c) 7.132   (d) 4.073

(e) 5.243   (f) 10.817   (g) 0.094   (h) 3.044

2 Which of the numbers below round off to 6.78 correct to two decimal places?

| 6.714 | | 6.769 | | 6.773 | | 6.782 | | 6.774 | | 6.786 |

3 Work out these answers on a calculator and then round off the answers correct to one decimal place.

(a) 0.49×5.7 (b) $3.71 \div 2.9$ (c) $\sqrt{26}$ (d) $38.14 \div 3.3$

4 Give these answers to two decimal places.

(a) $\sqrt{61}$ (b) 17.6×4.14 (c) 2.18^2 (d) $28.7 \div 5.92$

(e) $13.6 \div 7.3$ (f) $\dfrac{(28-9)^2}{1.73}$ (g) $\sqrt{86}$ (h) 46.13×2.89

HWK 1E ──────────────────────────────── **Main Book Page 45**

1 Work out these answers on a calculator and then round off the answers correct to two decimal places.

(a) $\dfrac{6.99}{2.01}$ (b) $\dfrac{3.8^2}{4.3}$ (c) $\dfrac{8.21}{\sqrt{53}}$ (d) $\dfrac{5.14 \times 3.6}{0.93}$

(e) $\dfrac{5.2}{1.9} + 8.714$ (f) $\dfrac{5.25}{(1.18 + 3.27)}$ (g) $\dfrac{5.06^2}{4.27}$ (h) $\dfrac{3.134}{2.6^2}$

2 Which number below is the smallest which will round off to 8.14 correct to two decimal places?

8.138   8.135   8.141   8.1354   8.1357   8.132

3 How many numbers below round off to 4.8 correct to one decimal place?

4.861   4.841   4.793   4.852   4.768   4.739

4 What is the smallest number which rounds off to 9.3 correct to one decimal place?

5 What is the smallest number which rounds off to 2.38 correct to two decimal places?

HWK 2M ──────────────────────────────── **Main Book Page 46**

1 Work out 40×20

2 Work out a rough estimate for 39×22

3 Work out 8×700

4 Work out a rough estimate for 7.93×706

5 Work out a rough estimate for 51×8.98

6 Do not use a calculator. Decide, by estimating, which of the three answers is closest to the exact answer.

	Calculation	A	B	C
(a)	7.3×31	2100	210	100
(b)	14.9×9.98	150	25	1500
(c)	24.8×40.2	100	1000	200
(d)	19.6×4.94	500	100	10
(e)	6.01×29.8	180	18	360
(f)	59.7×71.1	420	840	4200
(g)	$403 \div 79.12$	32000	50	5
(h)	$899 \div 1.98$	450	1800	45
(i)	$51 \div 0.99$	50	5	200
(j)	$607 \div 21.8$	3	120	30
(k)	$79.3 + 81 + 139$	300	200	400
(l)	9.6×90.4	450	900	90
(m)	$231 + 19.6 + 41.3$	200	390	290
(n)	19.7×31.06	60	300	600
(o)	$196 \div 51.3$	4	80	40

Do not use a calculator for these questions.

1 Gareth needs to buy 19 packets of cereal at £2.49 for each packet. Estimate the total cost.

2 A book weighs 292 g. Estimate how much 31 books would weigh?

3 A book costs £9.95. Estimate the cost of 152 books.

4 Write down each calculation below and match the correct answer from the list given.

    (a) $20.6 \div 5$ (b) 49×20.2 (c) 8.1×32 (d) 42×6.8

    (e) $2.8 + 13.9$ (f) $3012 \div 4.8$

| Answers: | 259.2 | 16.7 | 898.8 | 627.5 | 4.12 | 285.6 |

5 Caitlin covers 0.79 m every time she takes a stride. Estimate the distance she travels if she takes 994 strides.

6 Ryan sells cups of tea for 82p each from his stall. One weekend he sells 396 cups of tea. It costs him £130 to make the tea and sort out the cups. Estimate the profit he makes on selling cups of tea during this weekend.

7

box of paper	£4.95
ink cartridge	£13.10
pack of photo paper	£7.99

Louisa buys 3 boxes of paper, 2 ink cartridges and one pack of photo paper. Roughly how much change would Louisa get from £50?

2.2 Using algebra

1 Answer true or false.

    (a) $5m + 2m + 2n = 9mn$ (b) $5x + y + 3y = 5x + 4y$

    (c) $2p + 4 + 2p = 4p + 4$ (d) $4n - 2n + 3 = 5n$

Simplify the expressions in questions **2** to **10** by collecting like terms.

2 $3a + 4b + 2a$ **3** $8m + 3n + 4n - 4m$ **4** $2a + 5 + a + 1$

5 $4x + 3 - 2x - 1$ **6** $7w - 4w + 3 + 2w$ **7** $4m + 3m + 4n - 5m$

8 $7 + 4p - 3 - 3p$ **9** $5x - 2x + 6 - 5$ **10** $5a - a + 3 - 2a$

11 Find two matching pairs of expressions

A $\boxed{1 + 2m + 3}$ B $\boxed{2 + m + 4m - 1}$ C $\boxed{2 + 6m - 3m - 1}$

D $\boxed{7m + 1 - 2m}$ E $\boxed{5m + 4 - 3m}$

12 Find an expression for the total distance from A to C.

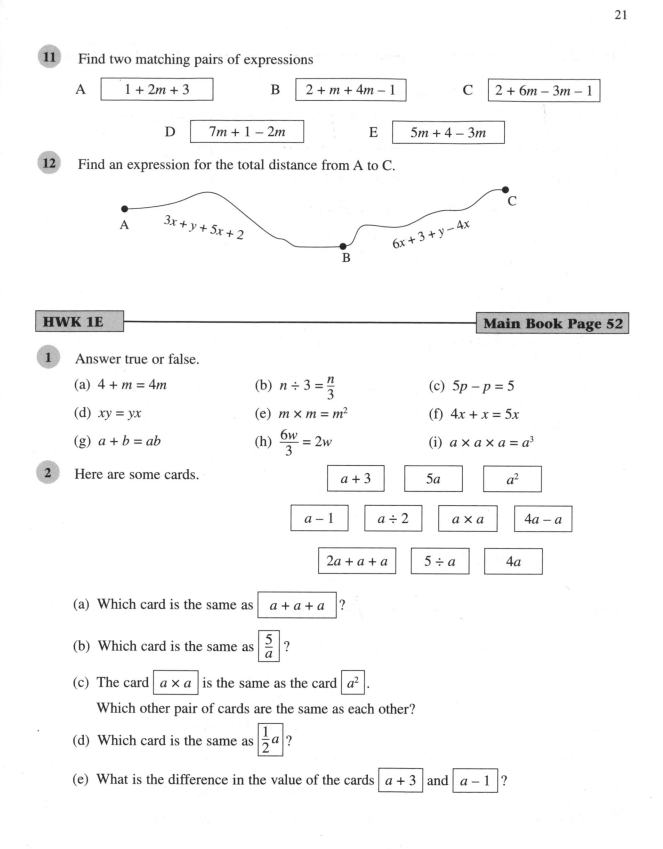

HWK 1E _____ **Main Book Page 52**

1 Answer true or false.

(a) $4 + m = 4m$ (b) $n \div 3 = \dfrac{n}{3}$ (c) $5p - p = 5$

(d) $xy = yx$ (e) $m \times m = m^2$ (f) $4x + x = 5x$

(g) $a + b = ab$ (h) $\dfrac{6w}{3} = 2w$ (i) $a \times a \times a = a^3$

2 Here are some cards.

$\boxed{a + 3}$ $\boxed{5a}$ $\boxed{a^2}$

$\boxed{a - 1}$ $\boxed{a \div 2}$ $\boxed{a \times a}$ $\boxed{4a - a}$

$\boxed{2a + a + a}$ $\boxed{5 \div a}$ $\boxed{4a}$

(a) Which card is the same as $\boxed{a + a + a}$?

(b) Which card is the same as $\boxed{\dfrac{5}{a}}$?

(c) The card $\boxed{a \times a}$ is the same as the card $\boxed{a^2}$.

Which other pair of cards are the same as each other?

(d) Which card is the same as $\boxed{\frac{1}{2}a}$?

(e) What is the difference in the value of the cards $\boxed{a + 3}$ and $\boxed{a - 1}$?

3 Tim has £(5n + 7). He buys a shirt for £(2n + 3). How much money does Tim now have?

4 Lily is running a (9w + 8) metre race. Write down an expression for how many more metres Lily has to run if she has completed (4w + 7) metres so far?

HWK 2M ──────────────────────── **Main Book Page 53**

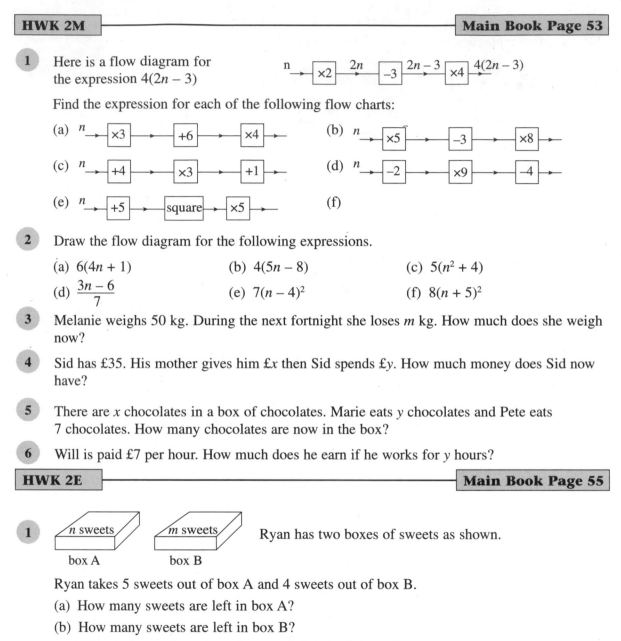

1 Here is a flow diagram for the expression 4(2n − 3)

$$n \xrightarrow{} \boxed{\times 2} \xrightarrow{2n} \boxed{-3} \xrightarrow{2n-3} \boxed{\times 4} \xrightarrow{4(2n-3)}$$

Find the expression for each of the following flow charts:

(a) $n \rightarrow \boxed{\times 3} \rightarrow \boxed{+6} \rightarrow \boxed{\times 4} \rightarrow$ (b) $n \rightarrow \boxed{\times 5} \rightarrow \boxed{-3} \rightarrow \boxed{\times 8} \rightarrow$

(c) $n \rightarrow \boxed{+4} \rightarrow \boxed{\times 3} \rightarrow \boxed{+1} \rightarrow$ (d) $n \rightarrow \boxed{-2} \rightarrow \boxed{\times 9} \rightarrow \boxed{-4} \rightarrow$

(e) $n \rightarrow \boxed{+5} \rightarrow \boxed{\text{square}} \rightarrow \boxed{\times 5} \rightarrow$ (f)

2 Draw the flow diagram for the following expressions.

(a) 6(4n + 1)   (b) 4(5n − 8)   (c) 5(n^2 + 4)

(d) $\dfrac{3n - 6}{7}$ (e) 7(n − 4)²   (f) 8(n + 5)²

3 Melanie weighs 50 kg. During the next fortnight she loses m kg. How much does she weigh now?

4 Sid has £35. His mother gives him £x then Sid spends £y. How much money does Sid now have?

5 There are x chocolates in a box of chocolates. Marie eats y chocolates and Pete eats 7 chocolates. How many chocolates are now in the box?

6 Will is paid £7 per hour. How much does he earn if he works for y hours?

HWK 2E ──────────────────────── **Main Book Page 55**

1 n sweets — box A   m sweets — box B   Ryan has two boxes of sweets as shown.

Ryan takes 5 sweets out of box A and 4 sweets out of box B.

(a) How many sweets are left in box A?

(b) How many sweets are left in box B?

(c) What is the total number of sweets left in both boxes?

(d) Ryan now puts one sweet back into box B. How many sweets are now in box B?

2 Mark has £n. Marcus has three times as much money as Mark. Marcus spends £15. How much money does Marcus now have?

3 In number walls each brick is made by adding the two bricks underneath it.

Draw the walls below and fill in the missing expressions.

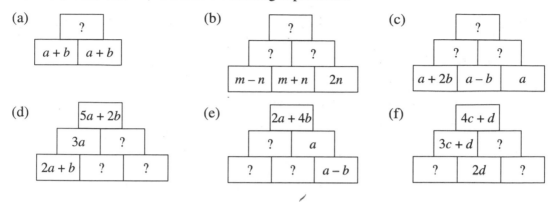

4 Felix has £(9n + 23). He spends £(3n + 9). He gives half of the remaining money to his sister. How much money does he have left?

2.3 Fractions, decimals, percentages

1 Answer true or false.

(a) $0.03 = \frac{3}{100}$ (b) $\frac{3}{5} = 0.35$ (c) $\frac{17}{20} = 0.85$

(d) $0.34 = \frac{3}{4}$ (e) $\frac{70}{100} = 0.7$ (f) $\frac{8}{25} = 0.32$

2 Change the following decimals to fractions, cancelling when possible.

(a) 0.2 (b) 0.09 (c) 0.36 (d) 0.75 (e) 0.007

(f) 0.025 (g) 0.73 (h) 0.008 (i) 0.45 (j) 0.16

3 Change the following fractions to decimals.

(a) $\frac{2}{5}$ (b) $\frac{11}{20}$ (c) $\frac{19}{50}$ (d) $\frac{13}{25}$ (e) $\frac{1}{8}$

4 For each pair of numbers, write down which is the larger.

(a) $\frac{7}{10}$ 0.8 (b) 0.94 $\frac{19}{20}$ (c) 0.17 $\frac{3}{20}$

(d) 0.26 $\frac{7}{25}$ (e) $\frac{3}{50}$ 0.04 (f) $\frac{9}{25}$ 0.49

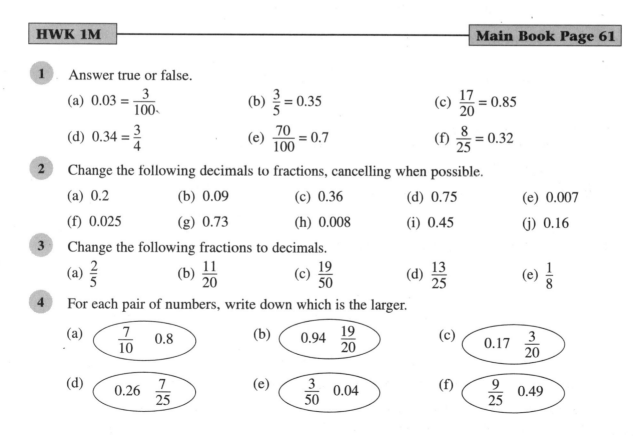

HWK 1E	Main Book Page 62

Change the following fractions to recurring decimals by dividing.

1 $\frac{1}{9}$ **2** $\frac{2}{7}$ **3** $\frac{1}{3}$ **4** $\frac{4}{7}$ **5** $\frac{1}{11}$

6 $\frac{6}{7}$ **7** $\frac{8}{9}$ **8** $\frac{4}{33}$ **9** $\frac{4}{11}$ **10** $\frac{2}{99}$

HWK 2M	Main Book Page 63

1

$\frac{7}{20}$	$\frac{6}{25}$	$\frac{9}{40}$	$\frac{1}{4}$

Change each fraction into a percentage then write these fractions in order of size, starting with the smallest.

2 Change these percentages to fractions.

(a) 41%   (b) 24%   (c) 6%   (d) 45%   (e) 32%

3 Change these percentages to decimals.

(a) 3%   (b) 30%   (c) 16%   (d) 75%   (e) 85%

4

Some people were asked what their favourite Disney cartoon was. The pie chart shows the results.

(a) What percentage prefer Snow White?

(b) What percentage prefer Jungle Book?

(c) What is the difference between the percentages for Jungle Book and the Lion King?

(d) What percentage prefer 'others'?

5 Change these decimals to percentages.

(a) 0.33   (b) 0.64   (c) 0.09   (d) 0.14   (e) 1.3

6 36% of people asked said they did not vote at the last General Election. What *fraction* of the people asked did vote in the last General Election?

80%	$\frac{12}{150}$	26%	$\frac{4}{5}$	16%	0.65	$\frac{15}{40}$	75%	$\frac{3}{25}$
0.48								0.08
0.75								$\frac{16}{20}$
$\frac{12}{25}$		Each number belongs to a group of 4						$\frac{3}{8}$
$\frac{13}{20}$		equivalent numbers (two fractions, one decimal and one percentage).						65%
0.34		Write down each group of 4 numbers.						$\frac{21}{28}$
$\frac{13}{50}$		Beware: there are 4 numbers which do *not* belong to any group.						$\frac{2}{25}$
37.5%								$\frac{39}{150}$
0.26	$\frac{36}{75}$	$\frac{12}{65}$	8%	$\frac{3}{4}$	0.8	48%	$\frac{52}{80}$	0.375

2.4 Geometrical Reasoning

Find the angles marked with letters.

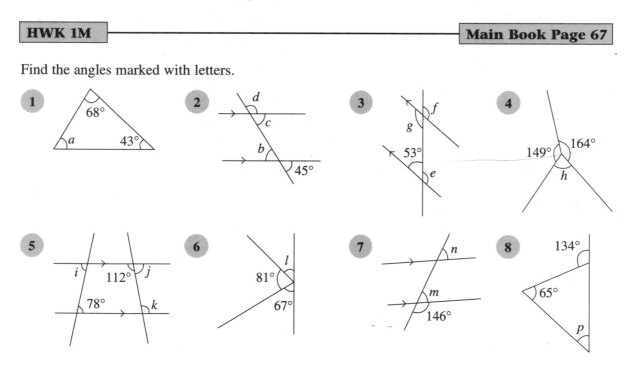

26

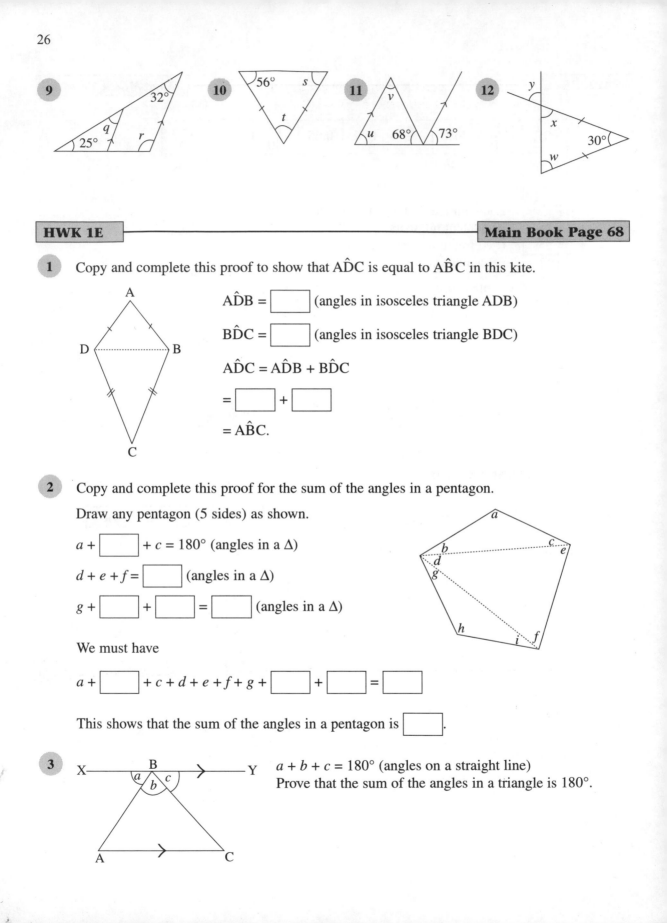

9 32° q 25° r

10 56° s t

11 v u 68° 73°

12 y x 30° w

HWK 1E ———————————————————— **Main Book Page 68**

1 Copy and complete this proof to show that AD̂C is equal to AB̂C in this kite.

A

D .... B

C

AD̂B = ☐ (angles in isosceles triangle ADB)

BD̂C = ☐ (angles in isosceles triangle BDC)

AD̂C = AD̂B + BD̂C

= ☐ + ☐

= AB̂C.

2 Copy and complete this proof for the sum of the angles in a pentagon.

Draw any pentagon (5 sides) as shown.

$a + $ ☐ $ + c = 180°$ (angles in a Δ)

$d + e + f = $ ☐ (angles in a Δ)

$g + $ ☐ $ + $ ☐ $ = $ ☐ (angles in a Δ)

We must have

$a + $ ☐ $ + c + d + e + f + g + $ ☐ $ + $ ☐ $ = $ ☐

This shows that the sum of the angles in a pentagon is ☐ .

3 X————B————→Y $a + b + c = 180°$ (angles on a straight line)
   a b c   Prove that the sum of the angles in a triangle is 180°.

A ——→ C

4 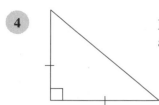 Prove that the angles in a right-angled isosceles triangle are 90°, 45° and 45°.

HWK 2M ——————————————————————— **Main Book Page 70**

Find the angles marked with letters.

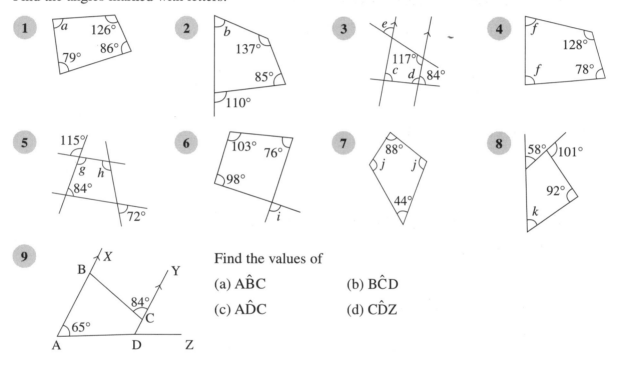

9

Find the values of

(a) AB̂C   (b) BĈD

(c) AD̂C   (d) CD̂Z

HWK 2E ——————————————————————— **Main Book Page 70**

Find the angles marked with letters.

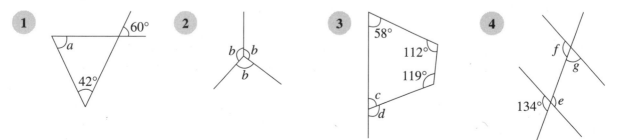

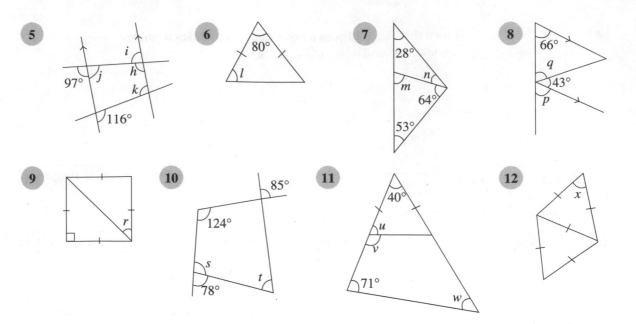

2.5 Construction and Locus

HWK 1M ───────────────────────────────── **Main Book Page 74**

You need a ruler, protractor and pair of compasses.

1 Construct triangle ABC as shown.
Use a protractor to measure AB̂C.

2 Construct each triangle and measure the side *x*.

(a)   (b)   (c)

3 Construct rhombus PQRS as shown.
Use a protractor to measure PQ̂R.

4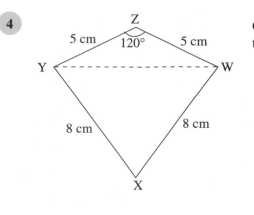

Construct the kite WXYZ. Use a protractor to measure WX̂Y.

Remember: The *locus* of a point is the path traced out by the point as it moves.

1 Mark a point A with a cross. Hundreds of ants stand *exactly* 6 cm from the point A. Draw a diagram to show this.

2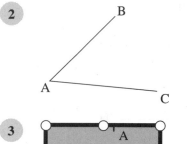

Copy this diagram. The ants now move so that each ant is *exactly* the same distance from line AB as line AC. Show this on your diagram.

3

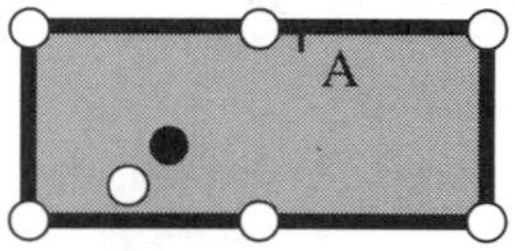

This diagram shows a white ball and black ball on a snooker table. Copy the diagram. Darryl hits the white ball against the black ball. The black ball hits the side of the table at A then goes down the hole in the bottom right-hand corner. Darryl is very surprised. Show what happens to the black ball on your diagram.

4 Draw another copy of the snooker table with the black ball in the same starting position. If the black ball goes down a different hole, show what happens to the black ball on your diagram.
Describe what happens to the black ball and which hole it goes down.

5

×   ×   ×   ×

×

                    ×

                ×

P ─────────────────── Q   · ×

                    ×

All the crosses shown above are 2.5 cm away from the line PQ. Copy the diagram and draw the locus of *all* the points 2.5 cm away from the line PQ.

6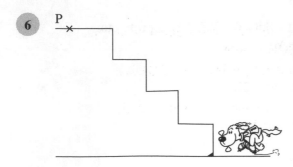

A dog with a bone in its mouth runs up these stairs and drops the bone on the point marked P.

Copy the stairs and draw a rough sketch of the locus of the bone as it travels from the bottom of the stairs to the point P.

HWK 2M/2E ──────────────────────────── **Main Book Page 76**

You need a ruler, protractor and pair of compasses.

1 Draw a horizontal line PQ of length 7 cm. Construct the perpendicular bisector of PQ.

2 Draw an angle of 60°. Construct the bisector of the angle.

3 (a) Construct the perpendicular bisector of a line AB as shown.
Label the bisector CD.
Label the point Y as shown.

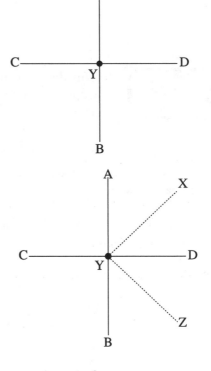

(b) Construct the bisector of $A\hat{Y}D$.

(c) Construct the bisector of $B\hat{Y}D$.

(d) Label the bisectors as shown opposite.

(e) Use your protractor to measure $C\hat{Y}X$.

(f) Use your protractor to measure $A\hat{Y}Z$.

4 Use a ruler and compasses only to construct an angle of $22\frac{1}{2}°$.

5

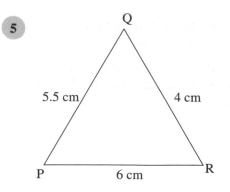

(a) Use a ruler and compasses only to construct triangle PQR as shown.

(b) Construct the angle bisector of QP̂R. Label this line PX.

(c) Construct the angle bisector of PR̂Q. Label this line RY.

(d) Use your protractor to measure QP̂X and PR̂Y.

2.6 Circles

HWK 1M ——————————————————— **Main Book Page 79**

For each of the circles shown below, write down
(a) the radius   (b) the diameter (you must give the units)

1 18 cm   **2** 4 m   **3** 6 m   **4** 13 mm   **5** 29 cm

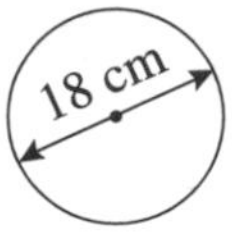

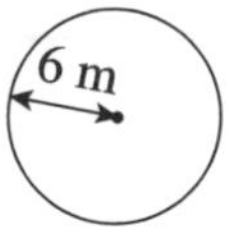

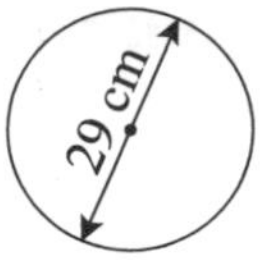

6 11 m   **7** 16 m   **8** 48 mm   **9** 9 cm   **10** 10.5 m

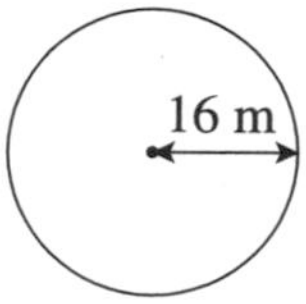

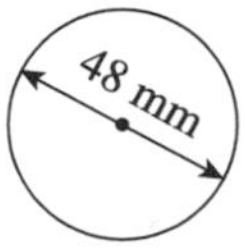

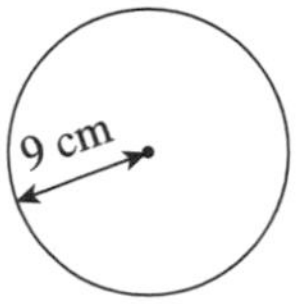

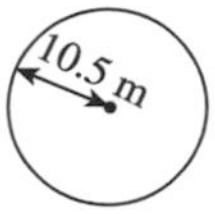

HWK 2M ——————————————————— **Main Book Page 81**

Remember: circumference = π × diameter

Give all answers to one decimal place.

1 Calculate the circumference of each circle.

(a) 8 cm   (b) 15 mm   (c) 3 m   (d) 7 m

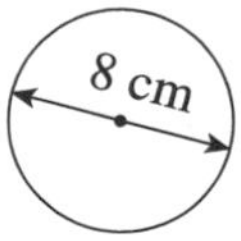

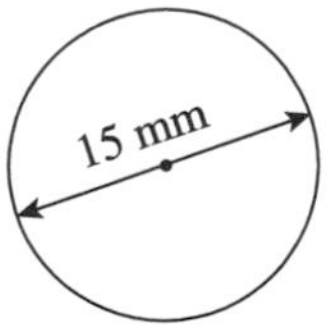

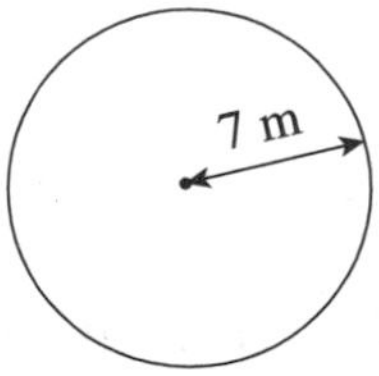

2 A circular pond has a diameter 30 m. Calculate its circumference.

3 A coin has a radius 8 mm. Find its circumference.

4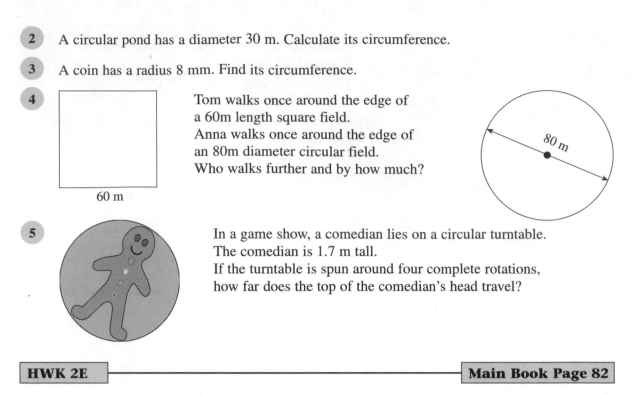

Tom walks once around the edge of a 60m length square field.
Anna walks once around the edge of an 80m diameter circular field.
Who walks further and by how much?

60 m

80 m

5 In a game show, a comedian lies on a circular turntable.
The comedian is 1.7 m tall.
If the turntable is spun around four complete rotations, how far does the top of the comedian's head travel?

HWK 2E ————————————————————————— **Main Book Page 82**

Calculate the perimeter of each shape. All shapes are either semi-circles or quarter circles. Give answers correct to 1 decimal place.

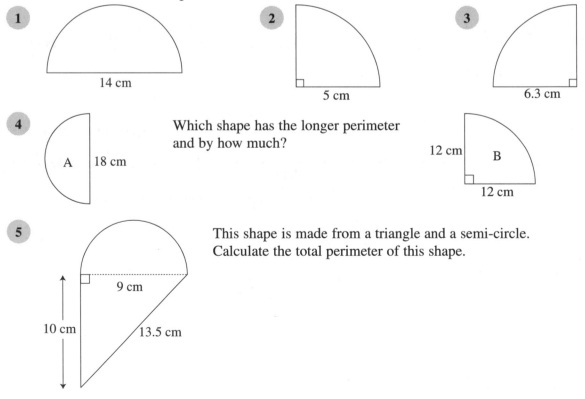

1 14 cm

2 5 cm

3 6.3 cm

4 A 18 cm

Which shape has the longer perimeter and by how much?

12 cm B

12 cm

5 This shape is made from a triangle and a semi-circle. Calculate the total perimeter of this shape.

9 cm

10 cm 13.5 cm

HWK 3M ——————————————————————— **Main Book Page 84**

Calculate the area of each circle and give your answer correct to one decimal place.

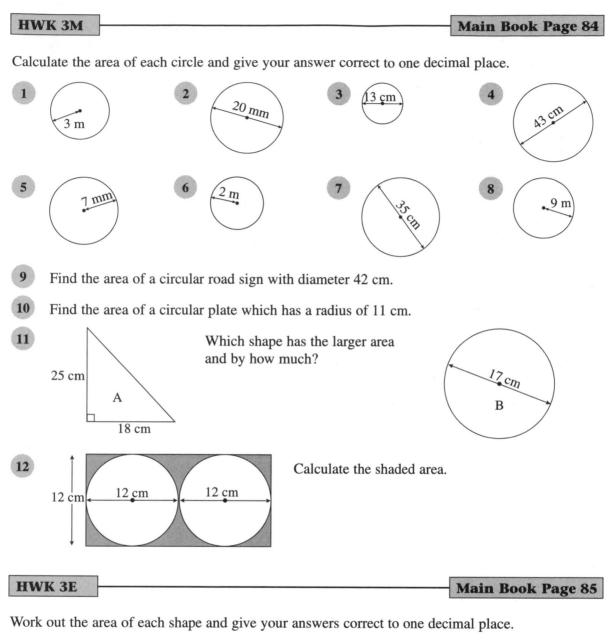

1 3 m

2 20 mm

3 13 cm

4 43 cm

5 7 mm

6 2 m

7 35 cm

8 9 m

9 Find the area of a circular road sign with diameter 42 cm.

10 Find the area of a circular plate which has a radius of 11 cm.

11 25 cm, 18 cm, A

Which shape has the larger area and by how much?

17 cm, B

12 12 cm, 12 cm, 12 cm

Calculate the shaded area.

HWK 3E ——————————————————————— **Main Book Page 85**

Work out the area of each shape and give your answers correct to one decimal place.

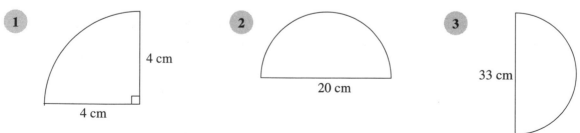

1 4 cm, 4 cm

2 20 cm

3 33 cm

4 A circular lawn has diameter 60 m. In the centre of the lawn is a circular pond with a radius of 5 m. What is the area of the lawn without the pond?

5

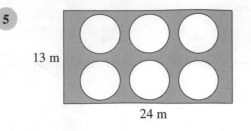

13 m

24 m

The shaded part of this design is to be painted blue. Each circle has a diameter of 7 m. Calculate the blue area.

6 This shape is made from a rectangle and a quarter circle. Calculate the total area of the shape.

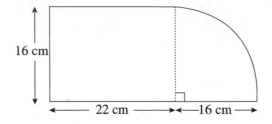

16 cm

22 cm   16 cm

UNIT 3

3.1 Written Calculations

HWK 1M — **Main Book Page 96**

Copy and complete this crossnumber *without using a calculator*.

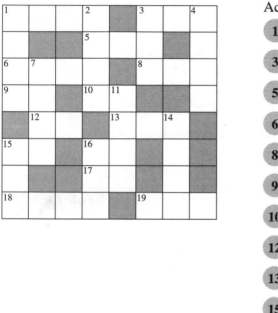

Across
1. 427×6
3. $9350 \div 10$
5. 68×6
6. 42×200
8. 30×25
9. $396 \div 6$
10. $672 \div 8$
12. $517 - 432$
13. $2422 \div 7$
15. $840 \div 12$
16. $928 \div 32$
17. $688 \div 43$
18. $5924 + 2450$
19. 161×5

Down
1. $3081 - 895$
2. 56×43
3. $1155 - 168$
4. 18×300
7. $2924 + 1756$
11. $6881 - 2485$
14. 231×30
15. $1117 - 389$
16. $1284 \div 6$

HWK 1E — **Main Book Page 97**

Work out, without a calculator

1. $68 \div 10$
2. 9.3×100
3. 0.169×1000
4. $0.25 - 0.142$
5. $94 \div 100$
6. $13.6 + 27$
7. $1.04 \div 4$
8. $0.392 \div 7$
9. 5.8×1000
10. $0.82 - 0.073$
11. $36 + 16.2$
12. $46 \div 1000$

36

13 | packet of crisps 48p
bottle of water £1.06
currant bun 39p | Sally buys 3 packets of crisps, 2 bottles of water and 2 currant buns. How much change will she get from £10?

14 How many currant buns in question **13** could you buy with £5?

15 Which is larger and by how much?

6.2 ÷ 1.00   or   0.8 – 0.739

16 100 'Calypso' chocolates cost £23.60. One thousand 'Midnight' chocolates cost £235. Which chocolate is the more expensive and by how much per chocolate?

17 Colin weighs 63.64 kg and Marie weighs 51.87 kg. How much heavier is Colin?

18 Charlie is sponsored 20p per kilometre for a charity run. How much money is he given if he runs 13.8 km?

HWK 2M —————————————————————— **Main Book Page 98**

For each of the scales work out the measurement shown by each arrow.

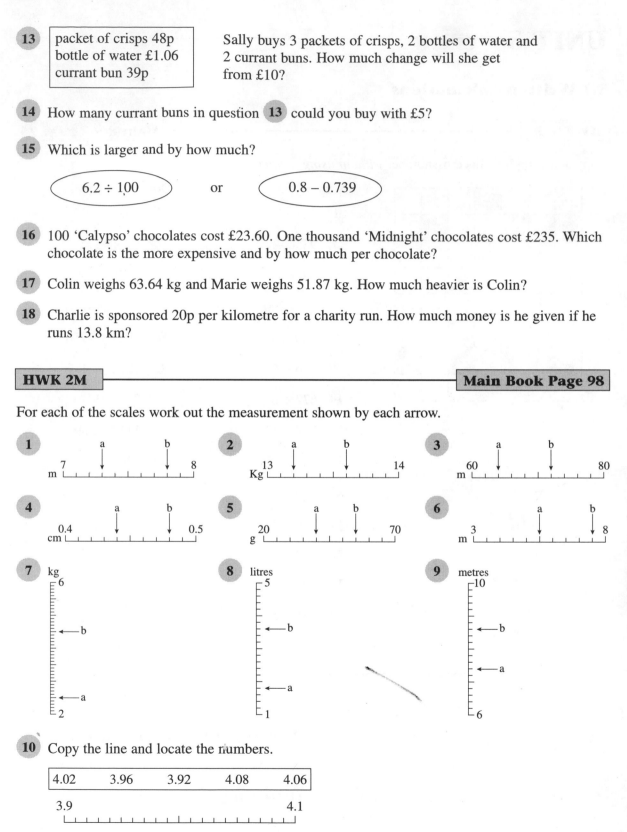

10 Copy the line and locate the numbers.

| 4.02 | 3.96 | 3.92 | 4.08 | 4.06 |

3.9   4.1

HWK 2E ──────────────────────────────── **Main Book Page 99**

1 Answer true or false.

(a) 0.08 > 0.6   (b) 0.74 > 0.069   (c) 0.063 > 0.261

(d) 0.19 < 0.51   (e) 0.006 > 0.0004   (f) 0.05 < 0.049

2 What has to be added or subtracted to change:

(a) 0.628 to 0.638   (b) 2.16 to 2.08   (c) 7.13 to 7.43

3 Six sprinters in a race record the times shown opposite.

(a) Who won the race?

(b) Who had the slowest time?

(c) Who finished in third place?

(d) How much faster was Kyle than Mike?

John	11.78 secs
Kyle	11.69 secs
Mike	11.8 secs
Wesley	11.05 secs
Shane	11.1 secs
Alan	11.96 secs

4 Arrange in order of size, smallest first.

(a) 0.52, 0.518, 0.5   (b) 0.821, 0.833, 0.83

(c) 0.06, 0.1, 0.102, 0.094   (d) 0.35, 0.324, 0.346, 0.32

5 Write down the next number in this sequence.

      3.03, 3.02, 3.01, 3, ?

HWK 3M ──────────────────────────────── **Main Book Page 100**

1 Work out

(a) 5×0.01 (b) 32×0.1 (c) 0.2×0.3 (d) 0.7×0.4

(e) 0.3×0.06 (f) 5×0.6 (g) 3×0.05 (h) 0.2×0.06

(i) 0.6×0.07 (j) 0.02×0.04 (k) 0.03×11 (l) 0.7×0.008

2 Answer true or false.

(a) $0.3^2 = 0.9$ (b) $0.1 \times 0.2 = 0.2$ (c) $0.5^2 = 0.25$

3 A four metre width of carpet costs £8.35 per metre. Calculate the cost of 6.4 m of carpet.

38

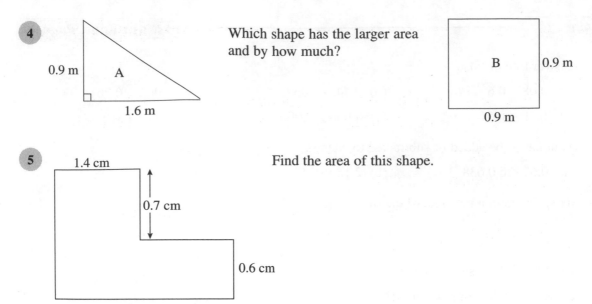

4 Which shape has the larger area and by how much?

A — 0.9 m, 1.6 m

B — 0.9 m, 0.9 m

5 Find the area of this shape.

1.4 cm
0.7 cm
0.6 cm
2.3 cm

HWK 3E | **Main Book Page 101**

1 Copy and complete the multiplication square.

×	0.3	0.05	7	1.2	0.9
0.6					
0.05					
1.1					
0.8					
4					

2 £1 can be changed for $1.46.

(a) How many dollars do you get for £300?

(b) How many dollars do you get for £550?

3 Ribbon costs £0.89 per yard. Jed buys 0.7 yards of ribbon. How much does this cost him? (Give your answer to the nearest penny)

4 Work out

(a) 0.26 × 1.3   (b) 2.9 × 0.017   (c) 0.81 × 5.3

HWK 4M   **Main Book Page 102**

1 Work out

(a) $8 \div 0.1$ (b) $43 \div 0.1$ (c) $0.6 \div 0.1$ (d) $7 \div 0.01$

(e) $0.2 \div 0.01$ (f) $22 \div 0.01$ (g) $58 \div 0.1$ (h) $0.9 \div 0.01$

2 How many 0.1 kg amounts of sugar can be obtained from 2.4 kg of sugar?

3 Answer true or false.

(a) $0.4 \div 0.01 = 4$ (b) $31 \div 0.1 = 310$ (c) $45 \div 0.01 = 450$

(d) $0.8 \div 0.01 = 800$ (e) $1 \div 0.01 = 100$ (f) $0.9 \div 0.1 = 9$

4 Find the missing numbers

(a) $14 \div \boxed{} = 1400$ (b) $5 \div \boxed{} = 50$ (c) $0.4 \div \boxed{} = 40$

(d) $\boxed{} \div 0.1 = 600$ (e) $3.6 \div \boxed{} = 36$ (f) $8.7 \div \boxed{} = 870$

HWK 4E   **Main Book Page 103**

1 Work out, without a calculator

(a) $6.39 \div 0.3$ (b) $0.72 \div 0.4$ (c) $0.49 \div 0.2$ (d) $1.158 \div 0.6$

(e) $3.78 \div 0.3$ (f) $0.1174 \div 0.02$ (g) $0.01352 \div 0.08$ (h) $9.52 \div 0.7$

(i) $0.0126 \div 0.09$ (j) $0.6656 \div 0.8$ (k) $0.01528 \div 0.002$ (l) $0.0655 \div 0.005$

2

A domino is 4.8 cm long. Hundreds of dominoes are laid in a line 1680 cm long. *Exactly* how many dominoes are used?

3 On average a chocolate raisin weighs 0.9 g. How many chocolate raisins will there be in a packet which weighs 76.5g?

4 Caroline works at a garage and is paid £8.20 per hour. Scott also works at the garage and is paid £7.50 per hour.

During one week, Caroline earns £164 and Scott earns £240. Work out the total number of hours Caroline and Scott worked for during that week.

Hidden words

(a) Start in the top left box.

(b) Work out the answer to the calculation in the box.

(c) Find the answer in the top corner of another box.

(d) Write down the letter in that box.

(e) Repeat steps (b), (c) and (d) until you arrive back at the top left box.

What is the message?

0.048	5.6	1.431	56	0.63	0.86
O	**E**	**E**	**N**	**T**	**T**
0.4×0.2	2.8×0.3	$28.8 \div 9$	$14 \div 1000$	$\frac{1}{2} + 0.35$	0.9×100
0.9	0.85	0.34	4.2	0.84	0.49
E	**O**	**U**	**E**	**F**	**T**
$86 \div 100$	$2.13 - 1.6$	0.7^2	$0.8^2 - 0.1^2$	7.2×1000	$1.9 + 3.7$
0.014	0.08	7200	90	0.53	3.2
O	**G**	**H**	**M**	**W**	**R**
$0.4 - 0.06$	$6.3 \div 7$	$0.631 + 0.8$	$448 \div 8$	0.4×0.12	0.6×7

3.2 Using a calculator

Work out, without a calculator. Show every step in your working.

1 $16 - 4 \times 2$

2 $20 \div 5 + 3$

3 $9 + 24 \div 6$

4 $41 - 12 \times 3$

5 $8 + 5 \times 2$

6 $(8 + 5) \times 2$

7 $9 \times (15 - 4)$

8 $6 + 6 \times 6$

9 $4 + 2 \times 6 - 3$

10 $(9 - 3) \times (4 + 5)$

11 $17 - 14 \div 2$

12 $5 \times (6 + 2 \times 2)$

13 $36 \div 9 - 22 \div 11$

14 $\dfrac{32}{5 + 3}$

15 $\dfrac{19 - 7}{8 - 2}$

16 Answer true or false.

(a) $(3 + 4)^2 = 49$

(b) $8^2 - 4 = 12$

(c) $8 + 3 \times 2 = 22$

(d) $5^2 - 3^2 = 16$

(e) $19 + 3 \times 4 = 31$

(f) $4 \times (6 + 3) = 27$

(g) $(4^2 + 2^2) \div 5 = 4$

(h) $\dfrac{25 - 8 \times 2}{3} = 3$

(i) $5 + 6^2 \div 9 = 9$

HWK 1E —————————————————————— **Main Book Page 107**

In questions **1** to **9** find the missing signs $(+, -, \times, \div)$. There are no brackets.

1 8 2 3 = 19

2 5 3 1 = 2

3 4 18 3 = 10

4 20 2 15 = 25

5 9 16 4 = 21

6 5 9 2 = 23

7 16 14 2 1 = 10

8 10 2 3 4 = 17

9 9 4 2 3 = 14

10 Copy each question and write brackets so that each calculation gives the correct answer.

(a) $6 + 3 \div 3 = 3$

(b) $8 - 2 \times 4 = 24$

(c) $9 + 1 \div 5 = 2$

(d) $3 \times 6 - 1 = 15$

(e) $28 \div 2 + 5 = 4$

(f) $8 + 3 \times 3 = 33$

(g) $5 + 20 \div 3 + 2 = 5$

(h) $30 - 20 - 15 = 25$

(i) $8 - 1 \times 10 - 3 = 49$

(j) $10 - 6 \div 1 + 3 = 1$

(k) $13 + 17 \div 5 = 6$

(l) $15 - 9 + 3 = 3$

HWK 2M —————————————————————— **Main Book Page 108**

Use a calculator and give answers correct to two decimal places. Remember BIDMAS.

1 $5.94^2 - 1.6$

2 $\dfrac{61}{4.7} + 3.9$

3 $5.3 + 2.9 \times 1.7$

4 $6.18 - 7 \div 13$

5 $13 \div 11 + 4.19$

6 $6.2 + \dfrac{4.3}{2.19}$

7 $8.24 + 15 \div 9.6$

8 $3.16^2 \div 27$

9 $3.51 - 2.17 \times 0.83$

10 $5.6 - \dfrac{16.4}{13}$

11 $5.12^2 \div 39$

12 $\dfrac{12.4 - 5.17}{2.3}$

13 $5.83 + 6.3 \times 2.19$

14 $\dfrac{8.3 + 16.14}{5.5}$

15 $1.739 + 4.7^2$

16 $\dfrac{2.6^2 + 1.35}{4.7}$

17 $16.14 - 0.38^2$

18 $\dfrac{(1.78 - 0.114)^2}{0.383}$

19 $6.3 \times (2.18 - 1.09)$

20 $\dfrac{1.17}{(0.68 + 0.23)^2}$

21 $\dfrac{1.16^2}{4.8^2}$

22 Jade sells security devices. She makes 8 selling trips to the north-west of England during one month. Each trip costs her £49.50. During the month she sells seven burglar alarms and 12 security spotlights. She makes £179 profit for each burglar alarm sold and £23 for each spotlight. How much money will she make in total during this month?

HWK 2E ———————————————————————————— **Main Book Page 109**

Work out, using a calculator ($a\frac{b}{c}$ button)

1 $\frac{5}{7} - \frac{1}{5}$ **2** $\frac{3}{4} \times \frac{7}{8}$ **3** $\frac{1}{6} + \frac{3}{11}$ **4** $\frac{6}{7} - \frac{3}{5}$

5 $\frac{4}{9} + \frac{3}{10}$ **6** $\frac{7}{10} + \frac{7}{8}$ **7** $3\frac{1}{4} - \frac{2}{3}$ **8** $2\frac{1}{2} + 1\frac{3}{5}$

9 $3\frac{1}{3} - 1\frac{1}{2}$ **10** $2\frac{3}{4} \times 1\frac{5}{6}$ **11** $4\frac{2}{5} \div 1\frac{1}{4}$ **12** $6\frac{1}{2} \div 2\frac{1}{6}$

13 Alana watches two films, one after the other. The first film lasts $1\frac{2}{3}$ hours and the second film lasts $2\frac{1}{10}$ hours. What is the total running time of both films?

14 A piece of timber is $3\frac{1}{4}$ m long. Terry uses two-thirds of the piece of timber. What length of timber does Terry use?

15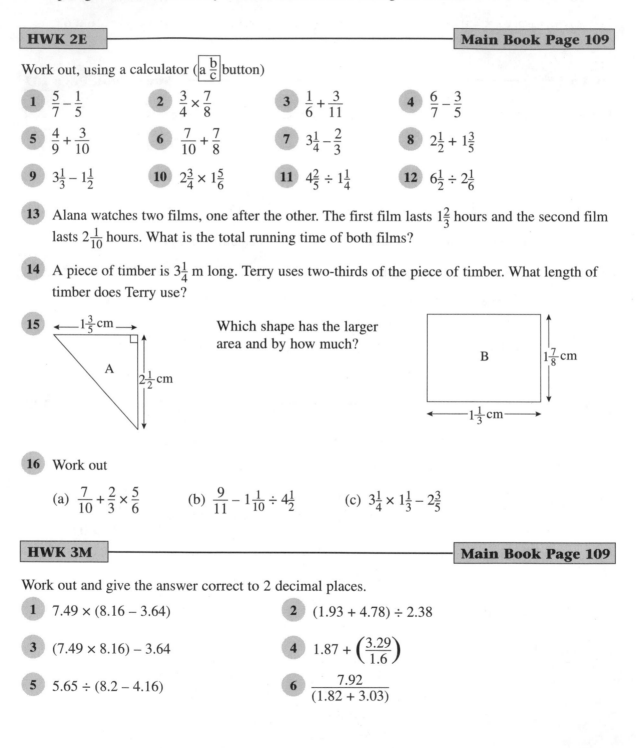

Which shape has the larger area and by how much?

16 Work out

(a) $\frac{7}{10} + \frac{2}{3} \times \frac{5}{6}$ (b) $\frac{9}{11} - 1\frac{1}{10} \div 4\frac{1}{2}$ (c) $3\frac{1}{4} \times 1\frac{1}{3} - 2\frac{3}{5}$

HWK 3M ———————————————————————————— **Main Book Page 109**

Work out and give the answer correct to 2 decimal places.

1 $7.49 \times (8.16 - 3.64)$ **2** $(1.93 + 4.78) \div 2.38$

3 $(7.49 \times 8.16) - 3.64$ **4** $1.87 + \left(\frac{3.29}{1.6}\right)$

5 $5.65 \div (8.2 - 4.16)$ **6** $\frac{7.92}{(1.82 + 3.03)}$

7 $\dfrac{(9.23 - 2.14)}{6.49}$

8 $0.18^2 \times 2.3$

9 $8.36 + 3.7^2$

10 $(3.62 + 2.59)^2$

11 $(7.12 + 4.93 - 1.86)^2 \times 1.6$

12 $\left(\dfrac{5.6}{1.93}\right) + 4.18$

13 $\dfrac{(11.6 - 3.14)}{(2.12 + 5.9)}$

14 $0.93^2 + 0.26^2$

15 $(5.1 \times 2.48) + (3.6 \times 2.9)$

16 $\dfrac{7.94}{2.16^2}$

17 $(8.29 - 2.11)^2$

18 $\dfrac{1.93^2}{(5.06 - 2.1)}$

19 $(7.62^2 \times 4.9) - 1.6^2$

20 $\dfrac{(8.62 + 3.59)}{(21.4 - 6.28)}$

HWK 3E — **Main Book Page 110**

Work out, using a calculator ($a\frac{b}{c}$ button)

1 $\dfrac{2}{3} \times \left(\dfrac{3}{4} - \dfrac{1}{5}\right)$

2 $\dfrac{9}{10} \div \left(\dfrac{3}{5} - \dfrac{3}{20}\right)$

3 $\left(\dfrac{4}{9} + \dfrac{2}{5}\right) \times \dfrac{3}{4}$

4 $\dfrac{5}{7} \times \left(2\dfrac{1}{4} - \dfrac{7}{8}\right)$

5 $\left(3\dfrac{1}{2}\right)^2 + \dfrac{5}{6}$

6 $4\dfrac{1}{4} \div 1\dfrac{1}{2} + \dfrac{5}{9}$

7 $\dfrac{2}{7} \times \dfrac{4}{5} + \dfrac{3}{8} \times \dfrac{2}{3}$

8 $\left(\dfrac{5}{8} - \dfrac{1}{3}\right)^2$

9 $\dfrac{\left(2\dfrac{1}{2} + 3\dfrac{2}{5}\right)}{\left(1\dfrac{1}{5} - \dfrac{5}{6}\right)}$

10 Copy and complete this multiplication table.

×		$\frac{1}{5}$	$2\frac{1}{4}$		
	$\frac{1}{2}$				
$1\frac{1}{3}$					
$\frac{7}{9}$	$\frac{14}{27}$			$\frac{35}{54}$	
		$\frac{4}{25}$			$\frac{2}{5}$
					$\frac{1}{3}$

Work out the following. Give each answer correct to one decimal place where appropriate.

1 $-9 \div (-2)$

2 $-18 - 14$

3 $-6.2 \times (-3.1)$

4 $4.8 - (-3.72)$

5 $-46 \div 4.13$

6 $(-8.12)^2$

7 $\dfrac{(-7) \times 2}{-5}$

8 $9 - 4.6^2$

9 $\dfrac{8 - (-0.17)}{2.3}$

10 $\left(\dfrac{-3.6}{1.92}\right) - (-2.8)$

11 $(-7.2 - 3.93)^2$

12 $49 - (-4.6)^2$

13 Copy and complete:

(a) $-3.7 + \boxed{} = 12.1$

(b) $5.17 + \boxed{} = -11.03$

(c) $\dfrac{-12.48}{\boxed{}} = -2.6$

(d) $4.3 \times \boxed{} = -29.24$

14 Which calculation gives the larger answer and by how much?

A $\boxed{(-4.9)^2 + 4.52}$

B $\boxed{(-5.2 + 10.31)^2 - 2.06}$

15 Which calculation gives the larger answer and by how much?

A $\boxed{\sqrt{(4.1 - (-8.15))}}$

B $\boxed{\dfrac{4.16 + (-1.9)^2}{2}}$

3.3 Formulas and expressions

In questions **1** to **10** you are given a formula. Find the value of the letter required in each case.

1 $a = 4b - 3$

Find a when $b = 5$

2 $p = 9w + 7$

Find p when $w = 6$

3 $y = 3x + 12$

Find y when $x = 5$

4 $m = \dfrac{n}{4} - 8$

Find m when $n = 48$

5 $a = \dfrac{b}{10} + 4$

Find a when $b = 30$

6 $y = 2(6x + 3)$

Find y when $x = 9$

7 $m = 7(4n - 1)$

Find m when $n = 6$

8 $a = \dfrac{8b - 4}{10}$

Find a when $b = 8$

9 $y = 3(9x + 2)$

Find y when $x = 2$

10 $p = \dfrac{w}{7} + 20$

Find p when $w = 28$

11 The perimeter of a rectangle is given by the formula $p = 2a + 2b$ where a is the length and b is the width.

Find the value of p when $a = 16$ and $b = 13$.

12 Gill is paid £m given by the formula $m = 8n + 42$, where n is the number of hours she works for. What is the value of m if she works for 30 hours?

13

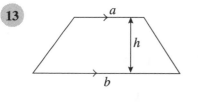

The area A of this trapezium is given by the formula

$$A = \frac{1}{2} h(a + b)$$

Find the value of A when $h = 10$, $a = 3$ and $b = 9$.

14

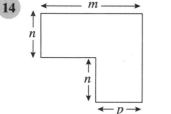

The \total area A of this shape is given by the formula
$$A = n(m + p)$$

Find the value of A when $n = 20$, $m = 40$ and $p = 15$.

HWK 1E ──────────────────────────── **Main Book Page 114**

1 In the formulas below x is given in terms of m and n. Find the value of x in each case.

(a) $x = 4m + 5n$ when $m = 6$ and $n = 3$

(b) $x = mn + 8m$ when $m = 5$ and $n = 7$

(c) $x = m^2 - 4n$ when $m = 9$ and $n = 20$

2 Using the formula $y = 17 + 9x$, find the value of y when

(a) $x = 7$ (b) $x = 0.1$ (c) $x = -0.1$

3 The surface area A of a sphere is approximately given by the formula
$A = 12r^2$

Find the surface area of a sphere with a radius of 4 cm.

4 Using the formula $m = 8(10 + n)$, find the value of m when

(a) $n = -4$ (b) $n = 20$ (c) $n = -10$

5 Norman sells chocolates. Each month he buys n boxes of chocolates to sell at £9 for each box. He always gives one box to his partner and one box to each of his two children. Norman gets £m for selling the remaining boxes given by the formula

$$m = 9(n - 3)$$

Find the value of m when

(a) $n = 43$ (b) $n = 60$ (c) $n = 100$

6 Using the formula $I = \dfrac{PTR}{100}$, find the value of I when P = 400, T = 3 and R = 9.

7 This open box has no top.

The surface area A is given by the formula
$A = 2np + mn + 2mp$
Find the value of A when $m = 8$, $n = 6$ and $p = 3$.

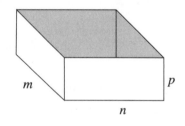

HWK 2M   **Main Book Page 116**

1 Find the values of these expressions when $n = 6$.

(a) $\dfrac{3n + 12}{n}$ (b) $\dfrac{n + 2}{n - 2}$ (c) $5(3n - 1)$

2 Find the value of each expression.

(a) $4n - 3$ if $n = 7$ (b) $6y + 2$ if $y = 9$ (c) $8 - 2x$ if $x = 3$

(d) $5n - 9$ if $n = 15$ (e) $\dfrac{x}{5} + 4$ if $x = 40$ (f) $3(4 + 2y)$ if $y = 10$

(g) $n^2 - 19$ if $n = 8$ (h) $\dfrac{4x}{3} - 16$ if $x = 12$

3 Find the values of these expressions when $m = 7$.

(a) $\dfrac{2m}{14}$ (b) $11m - 52$ (c) $100 - m^2$

4 Which of the cards below have a value of 15 when $x = 4$?

| $3x + 4$ | $x^2 - 1$ | $20 - x$ | $(x - 1)^2 + 6$ |

| $\dfrac{30x}{8}$ | $2x + 9$ | $5x - 5$ |

HWK 2E ——————————————————————————— **Main Book Page 117**

In questions **1** to **16** find the value of the expressions given that $a = 5$ $b = -3$ $c = 2$

1 $a + b$ **2** c^2 **3** b^2 **4** $c - b$

5 $2a + 1$ **6** $c + b$ **7** $4(a - b)$ **8** $b^2 + 7$

9 $\dfrac{4b}{c}$ **10** $\dfrac{3a + 3}{2b}$ **11** $4b - 1$ **12** bc

13 $\dfrac{5c - 5b}{a}$ **14** abc **15** $a(2c + b)$ **16** $3ab$

17 If $n = -2$, which expression has the larger value?

| $5n - n$ | or | $2(4n + 3)$ |

18 For each statement answer 'true' or 'false'

(a) $m - n = n - m$ (b) $5m - m = 5$ (c) $m \times m = m^2$

(d) $m + m + m = 3m$ (e) $6m + m = 7m$ (f) $m \div 3 = 3 \div m$

19 Given that $w = -5$ and $x = 9$, find the value of each of the following expressions.

(a) $x - w$ (b) $x^2 + w$ (c) $4(w + x)$ (d) xw (e) $2w + x$

(f) $w^2 + 3$ (g) $x(3x + w)$ (h) $\dfrac{10x}{w}$ (i) $w(2x - w)$

3.4 Drawing graphs

HWK 1M ——————————————————————————— **Main Book Page 120**

Look at the grid at the top of the next page to answer these questions.

1 Write down the coordinates of points M and F.

2 B lies on the line $y = 3$. Which line does the letter K lie on?

3 Which letters lie on the line $x = 1$?

4 Which letter lies on $x = 7$?

5 Which letters lie on $x = 5$?

6 Which letter lies on $y = 6$?

7 Which letter lies on $x = 4$?

8 Letter G lies on $x = 5$ and $y = 5$.
What letter lies on $x = 2$ and $y = 6$?

9 What letter lies on $x = 6$ and $y = 7$?

10 What letter lies on $x = 1$ and $y = 2$?

11 Which line passes through G and L?

12 Which line passes through E, N and D?

HWK 1E ———————————————————————— **Main Book Page 121**

1 Write down the co-ordinates of points C and K.

2 Letter J lies on the line $x = 1$. Which other letters lie on this line?

3 Letter E lies on the line $y = -4$. Which other letters lie on this line?

4 Which letters lie on the line $y = 1$?

5 Which letters lie on the line $x = -4$?

6 Which line passes through the letters B and I?

7 Which line passes through the letters K and J?

8 Write down the equation of the horizontal broken line.

9 What letter lies on $x = -4$ and $y = -2$?

10 What letter lies on $x = -2$ and $y = 1$?

11 Write down the equation of the vertical broken line?

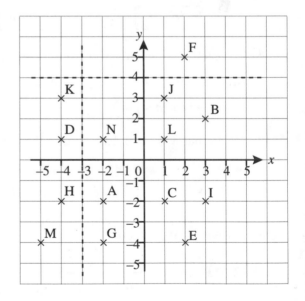

(There are 3 more questions on the next page)

12 Write down the equation of the horizontal line which passes through four of the letters shown.

13 Which two lines meet at the point F?

14 Which two lines meet at the point A?

HWK 2M ──────────────────────────── **Main Book Page 123**

For each question, copy and complete the table then draw the graph using the scales given.

1 $y = 2x + 2$ for x-values from 0 to 5

$2x + 2$ means $\boxed{x} \rightarrowtail \boxed{\times 2} \rightarrowtail \boxed{+2}$

x	0	1	2	3	4	5
y					10	
coordi-nates					(4, 10)	

(x-axis: use 1 cm for 1 unit
y-axis: use 1 cm for 2 units)

2 $y = 5 - x$ for x-values from 0 to 5

$5 - x$ means $\boxed{5} \rightarrowtail \boxed{-x}$

x	0	1	2	3	4	5
y			3			
coordi-nates			(2, 3)			

(x-axis: 1 cm for 1 unit
y-axis: 1 cm for 1 unit)

3 $y - 3x + 1$ for x-values from 0 to 5

$3x + 1$ means $\boxed{x} \rightarrowtail \boxed{\times 3} \rightarrowtail \boxed{+1}$

(x-axis: 1 cm for 1 unit, y-axis: 1 cm for 2 units)

4 $y = \frac{1}{2}x + 2$ for x-values from 0 to 6

$\frac{1}{2}x + 2$ means $\boxed{x} \rightarrowtail \boxed{\times \frac{1}{2}} \rightarrowtail \boxed{+2}$

(x-axis: 1 cm for 1 unit, 2 cm for 1 unit)

50

1 Using the same axes, draw the graphs of
$y = 3x - 1$, $y = 3x - 3$, $y = 3x$ and $y = 3x + 3$.
Write down what you notice about each line and its equation.
(Clues: where do the lines cut the y-axis? – are the lines parallel?)

2 Three of the lines below are parallel. Write down the equation of the line which is *not* parallel to the other lines.

$$y = 4x + 1 \qquad y = 3x + 4 \qquad y = 4x - 2 \qquad y = 4x + 4$$

3 Draw the graph of $y = x^2 + 2$ using x-values from 0 to 4.

1 The temperature in a house was recorded every two hours for a whole day; the results are shown below.

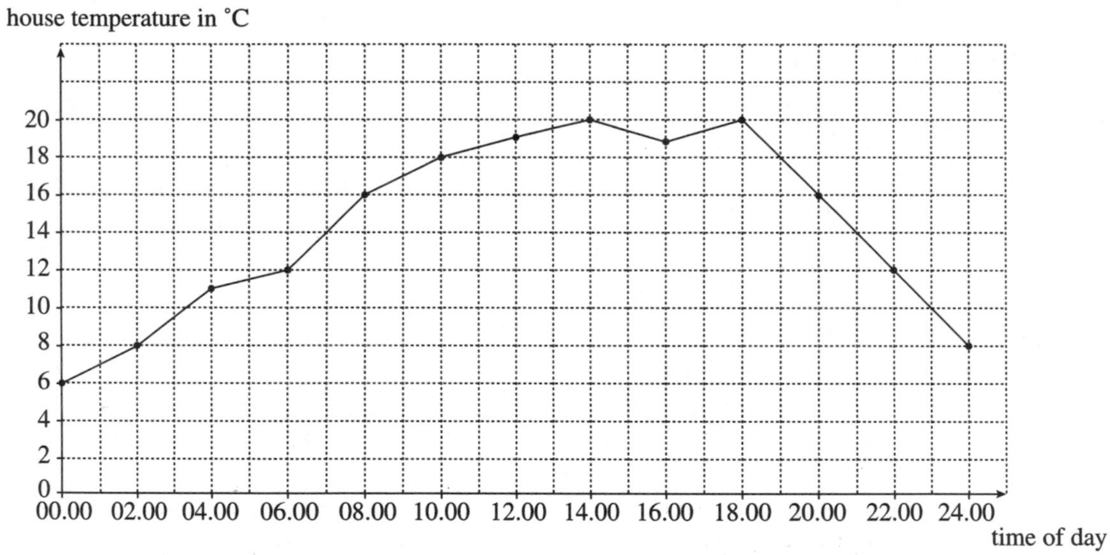

house temperature in °C

(a) What was the temperature at 10.00 h?

(b) What was the temperature at 20.00 h?

(c) What was the temperature at 02.00 h?

(d) At which two times was the temperature 16°C?

(e) At which two times was the temperature 20°C?

(f) What was the temperature at 23.00 h?

2 One gallon is approximately 4.5 litres.

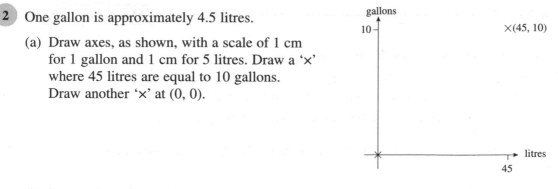

(a) Draw axes, as shown, with a scale of 1 cm for 1 gallon and 1 cm for 5 litres. Draw a 'x' where 45 litres are equal to 10 gallons. Draw another 'x' at (0, 0).

(b) Draw a long straight line through the two points above and use your graph to convert:

   (i) 2 gallons into litres   (ii) 37.5 litres into gallons

(c) Ben puts 13.5 litres of petrol into his car. This costs him £15.45. Use your graph to help you calculate the cost of 1 gallon of petrol.

3 A man climbing a mountain measures his height above sea level after every 30 minutes; the results are shown below.

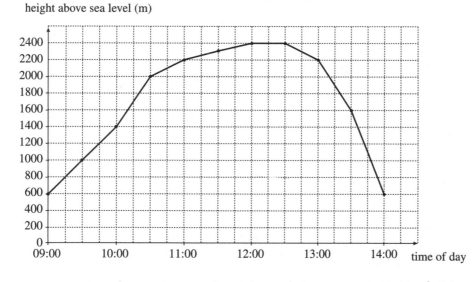

(a) At what height was he at 10:00 h?

(b) At what height was he at 13:30 h?

(c) Estimate his height above sea level at 09:45 h.

(d) Estimate his altitude at 10:45 h.

(e) Estimate his height above sea level at 13:45 h.

(f) At what two times was he 2200m above sea level?

(g) How high was the mountain? (He got to the top!)

(h) How long did he rest at the summit?

(i) How long did he take to reach the summit?

52

In questions **1** to **10** you are given the coordinates of several points on a line. Find the equation of each line.

1

x	1	2	3	4	5
y	5	6	7	8	9

2

x	1	2	3	4	5
y	10	11	12	13	14

3

x	9	8	7	6	5
y	5	4	3	2	1

4

x	5	6	7	8	9
y	4	3	2	1	0

5

x	1	2	3	4	5
y	5	10	15	20	25

6

x	4	5	6	7	8	9
y	19	20	21	22	23	24

7

x	10	12	14	16	18
y	4	6	8	10	12

8

x	20	19	18	17	16
y	0	1	2	3	4

9

x	2	4	6	8	10
y	16	32	48	64	80

10

x	1	2	3	4	5
y	1	3	5	7	9

11

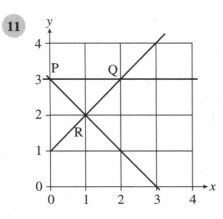

Find the equation of the line through

(a) R and Q

(b) P and Q

(c) P and R

3.5 Reflection

HWK 1M **Main Book Page 130**

Copy each shape on squared paper and draw the image after reflection in the broken line.

1
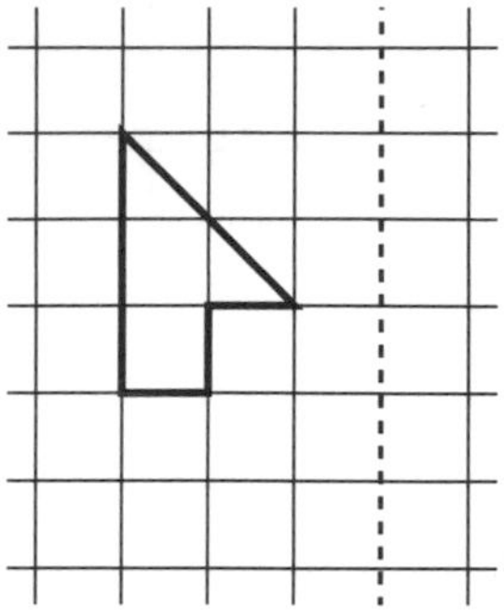

2
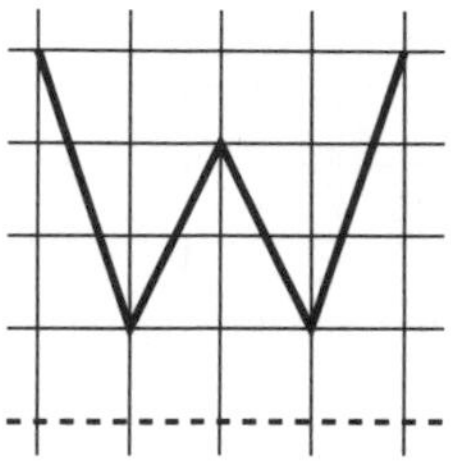

3
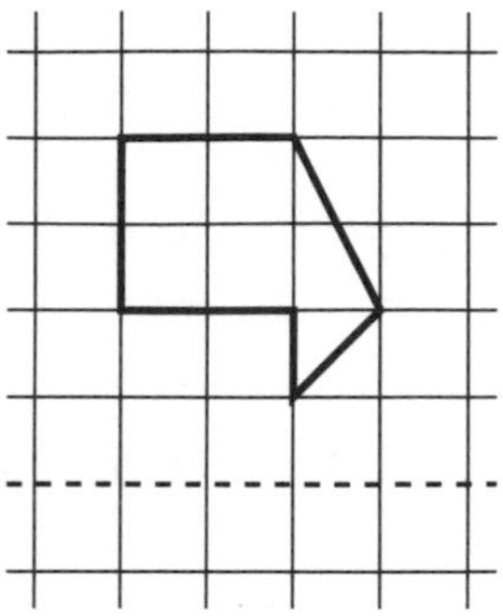

4
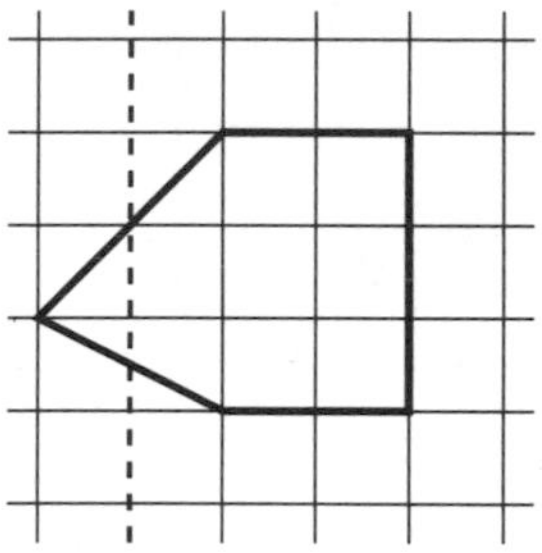

5
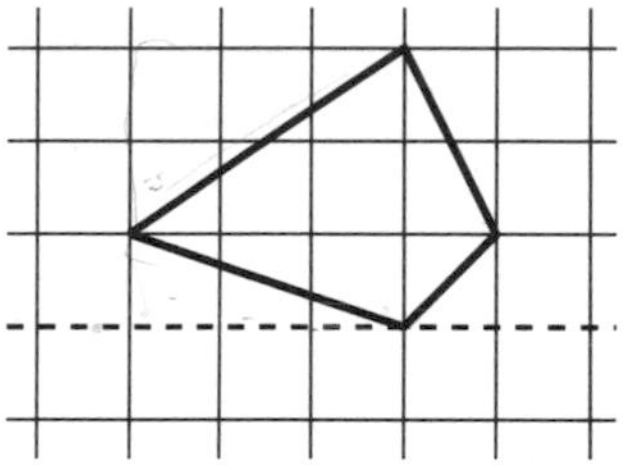

6
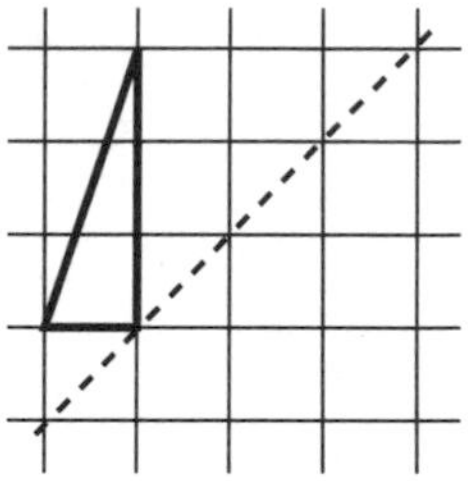

7
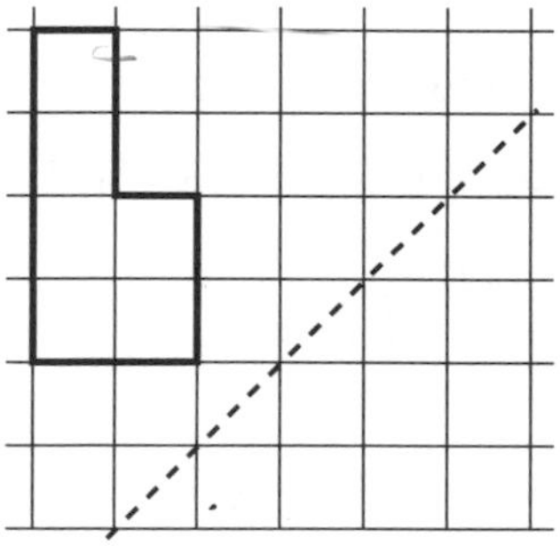

8
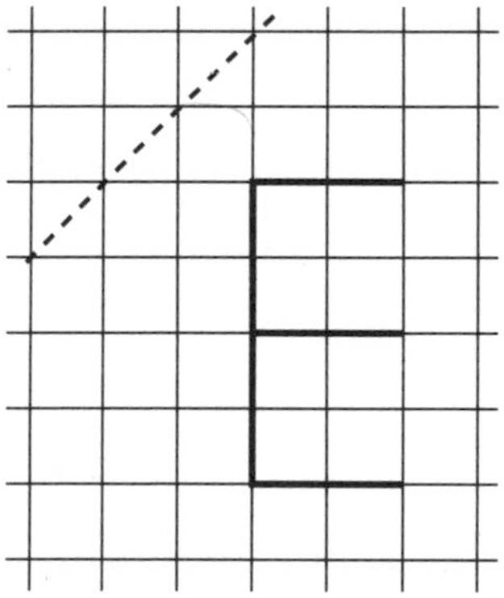

9
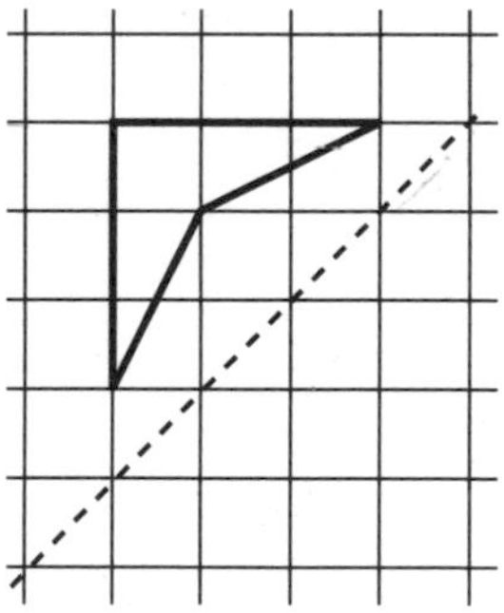

10 Draw any quadrilateral (4-sided shape) and reflect it in a diagonal line.

In questions **1** to **3** , copy each shape and draw the image after reflection in the broken line.

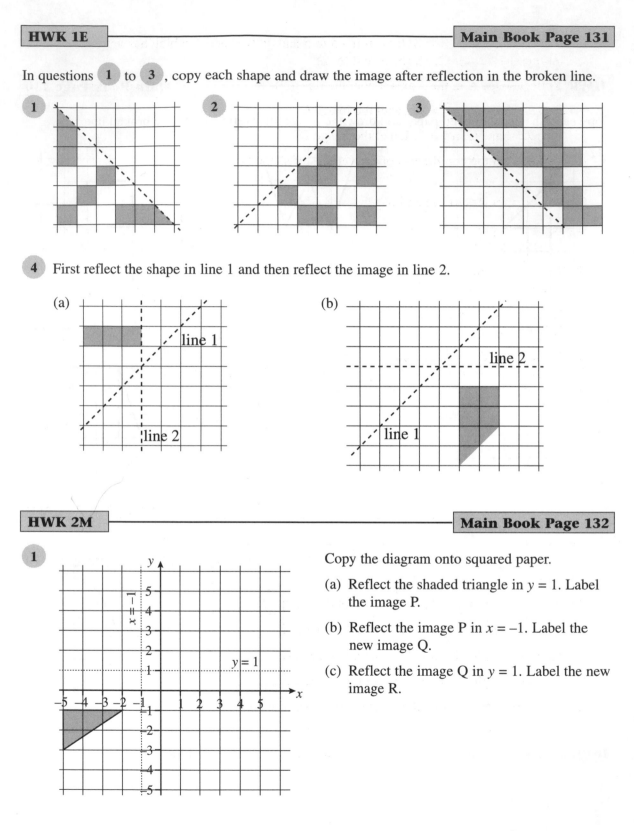

4 First reflect the shape in line 1 and then reflect the image in line 2.

1

Copy the diagram onto squared paper.

(a) Reflect the shaded triangle in $y = 1$. Label the image P.

(b) Reflect the image P in $x = -1$. Label the new image Q.

(c) Reflect the image Q in $y = 1$. Label the new image R.

2 (a) Draw x and y axes with values from -5 to 5 and draw shape A which has vertices (corners) at $(2, 2)$, $(2, 3)$, $(5, 3)$ and $(5, 2)$.

(b) Reflect shape A in the x axis. Label the image B.

(c) Reflect shape B in $x = 1$. Label the image C.

(d) Reflect shape C in $y = 1$. Label the image D.

(e) Write down the coordinates of the vertices of shape D.

3 Copy the diagram onto squared paper.

(a) Reflect triangle P in $y = x$.
Label the image Q.

(b) Reflect triangle Q in $x = 2$.
Label the image R.

(c) Reflect triangle R in the x-axis.
Label the image S.

(d) Write down the coordinates
of the vertices of triangle S.

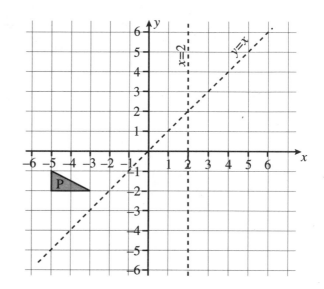

HWK 2E —————————————————————— **Main Book Page 134**

1 (a) Draw x and y axes with values from -5 to 5 and draw triangle A which has vertices at $(2, -1)$, $(2, -4)$ and $(3, -4)$.

(b) Reflect triangle A in the y-axis. Label the image B.

(c) Reflect triangle B in $y = -1$. Label the image C.

(d) Reflect triangle C in $x = 1$. Label the image D.

(e) Reflect triangle D in $y = x$. Label the image E.

(f) Write down the coordinates of the vertices of triangle E.

2

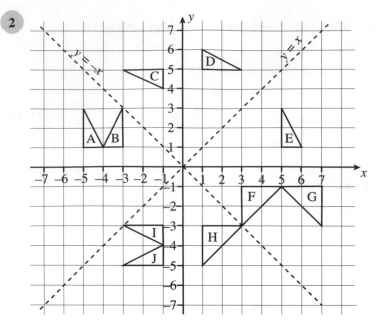

Write down the equation of the mirror line for each of the following reflections.

(a) A → B

(b) B → E

(c) I → J

(d) D → E

(e) A → C

(f) C → J

(g) H → F

(h) F → G

UNIT 4

4.1 Describing data

HWK 1M — **Main Book Page 148**

1 5 6 13 8 6 5 8 4 10 4 8

For the list of numbers above, find

(a) the mean (b) the median (c) the mode (d) the range

2 The numbers below show the scores of ten golfers.

–3, –1, –5, +2, +3, –6, –4, –3, +2, –4

Write down the median score.

3 Which set of numbers below has the greater range?

A 5, –2, 9, 3, –1, 8 or B –6, 2, –2, 5, –3, 6, –4

4 Nine people have weights 52 kg, 63 kg, 51 kg, 48 kg, 62 kg, 59 kg, 60 kg, 62 kg and 56 kg.

(a) Find the mean weight of the nine people.

(b) Two more people join the group. They weigh 79 kg each. Find the mean weight of all eleven people.

5 Eight people each have one money note as shown below.

20 10 10 20

5 20 5 10

Find the mean average amount of money each person has.

HWK 1E — **Main Book Page 149**

1 3 7 ? 10

The numbers on these cards have a mean average equal to 6.
Write down the missing number.

2 The numbers 7, 4, 9, 2, 7 and n have a median equal to 6. Write down the value of n.

58

3 Nine children get the following marks in a test:

36, 50, 54, 59, 37, 62, 52, 51, 49

Gemma scored the mean average mark. Was she in the bottom half or the top half of this list of marks?

4 Set A: | 8 | 10 | 5 | 9 | 6 | 7 | 4 |

Set B: | 12 | 1 | ? | 8 | 9 |

The mean average of set B is the same as the mean average of set A.
Find the missing number.

5 The six numbers below are all positive and have a range of 39. Find the value of *n*.

(15) (21) (3) (*n*) (32) (9)

6 Seven numbers have a mean of 9 and a median of 8.

| 6 | 6 | 15 | 15 | ☐ | ☐ | ☐ |

Write down three possible missing numbers.

HWK 2M — **Main Book Page 150**

1 Children in class 8A are given a maths test. Their marks are recorded below.

| 17 | 23 | 19 | 28 | 15 | 17 | 22 | 28 | 19 | 20 |
| 24 | 8 | 21 | 15 | 28 | 16 | 27 | 29 | 21 | 23 |

(a) Find the mean mark and the range of the marks.

(b) Children in class 8B took the same test. Their mean mark was 24 and the range of the marks was 12. Use the means and the ranges to compare the test marks for classes 8A and 8B.

2 Two groups of people were asked to estimate when one minute had passed. Their estimates are shown in the boxes below. The times are given in seconds.

| Group X | 54 | 61 | 60 | 55 | 62 | 66 | 61 | 51 | 52 |
| Group Y | 59 | 58 | 67 | 50 | 63 | 69 | 71 | 67 |

(a) Work out the mean estimate and the range for group X.

(b) Work out the mean estimate and the range for group Y.

(c) Write one or two sentences to compare the estimates for the two groups.

You may use a calculator.

1   The frequency table shows the weights of 50 apples in a box.

weight	90 g	100 g	110 g	120 g	130 g
frequency	8	11	17	9	5

(a) Calculate the mean weight of the apples.

(b) Find the modal weight of the apples (ie. the mode).

2   40 children were asked how many drinks of water they had during one day. The findings are shown in the frequency table below.

number of drinks	0	1	2	3	4	5	6
frequency	3	5	6	7	12	5	2

(a) Calculate the mean number of drinks.

(b) Find the modal number of drinks (i.e. the mode).

3   Tom wants to know if a 'city' family or a 'village' family spends more or less each week on food. He asks 25 families in a city and 25 families in a village. The results are shown in the frequency tables below.

city		village	
food bill (£)	frequency	food bill (£)	frequency
80	0	80	5
100	4	100	5
120	8	120	10
140	6	140	4
160	7	160	1

(a) Calculate the mean weekly food bill for the 'city' families.

(b) Calculate the mean weekly food bill for the 'village' families.

(c) Which group of families spends more each week on food. Can you suggest a possible reason for this?

HWK 3M/3E — **Main Book Page 154**

1. 25 people are asked how many DVDs they have. The results are shown below.

15	21	41	43	38
8	23	34	47	16
22	38	43	20	6
33	21	19	8	23
34	12	43	16	37

Draw an ordered stem and leaf diagram.
Three entries are shown below.

Stem	Leaf
0	
1	2
2	0
3	3
4	

Remember the key, for example: 1|2 means 12

2. The numbers shown below give the ages of 30 people on a train between Birmingham and Derby. Draw an ordered stem and leaf diagram to show this data.

24	48	17	58	52	40	64	57	69	28
67	58	32	66	13	68	59	37	10	66
63	21	19	48	57	69	17	58	67	24

3. The stem and leaf diagrams below show the weights of the players in two rugby teams.

<u>Halford</u>

Stem	Leaf
8	3 8 9
9	2 5 6 6 8
10	6 7 7
11	3 4 6
12	1

Key
9|5 means 95 kg

<u>Malby</u>

Stem	Leaf
8	0 2
9	4 8 9
10	6 7 7 7
11	2 5 5 8
12	4 9

Key
10|7 means 107 kg

(a) Find the range and median weight of the rugby players for each team.

(b) Write two sentences to compare the weights of the rugby players in each team (One sentence should involve how spread out the weights are (range) and the second sentence should involve an average (median)).

4   A group of children are drawing with pencils.
    The stem and leaf diagram opposite shows
    the length of each pencil.

    (a) What is the median pencil length?

    (b) Write down the range.

Stem	Leaf
7	4 6
8	3 5 5
9	0 2 4 4 7
10	2 6 7 7
11	4 5 8 8 8
12	3 4 5 5 9 9
13	2 2 6 7

Key
9|4 means 9.4 cm

4.2 Rotation and combined transformations

HWK 1M ———————————————————————— **Main Book Page 156**

In questions **1** to **6** draw the shape and then draw and shade its new position
(the image). Take 0 as the centre of rotation in each case.

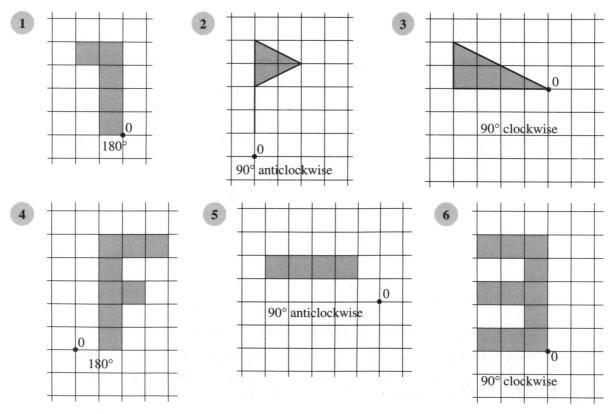

1   180°

2   90° anticlockwise

3   90° clockwise

4   180°

5   90° anticlockwise

6   90° clockwise

HWK 1E

Main Book Page 157

1 Copy the diagram shown, using axes from –6 to 6.

(a) Rotate shape P 90° anticlockwise about (0, 0). Label the new shape R.

(b) Rotate triangle Q 90° clockwise about (4, –1). Label the new shape S.

(c) Rotate shape Q 180° about (0, 0). Label the new shape T.

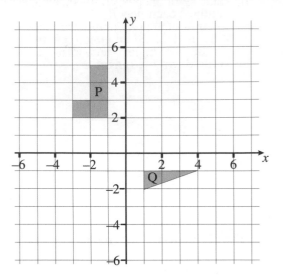

2 (a) Draw axes with values from –6 to 6 and draw triangle P with vertices at (–3, –2), (–3, –6) and (–5, –2).

(b) Rotate triangle P 90° anticlockwise about (0, 0). Draw and label the new triangle Q.

(c) Rotate triangle Q 90° anticlockwise about (2, –2). Draw and label the new triangle R.

(d) Rotate triangle R 180° about (3, 2). Draw and label the new triangle S.

(e) Rotate triangle S 90° anticlockwise about (0, 0). Draw and label the new triangle T. Write down the co-ordinates of each vertex (corner) of triangle T.

HWK 2M

Main Book Page 158

In questions **1** and **2** copy each diagram. Use tracing paper to find the centre of each rotation.

1

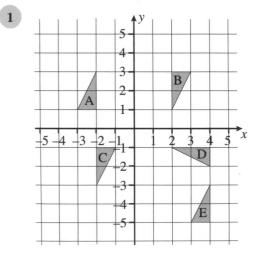

(a) rotation of ΔA onto ΔB

(b) rotation of ΔA onto ΔC

(c) rotation of ΔB onto ΔD

(d) rotation of ΔC onto ΔE

2 (a) rotation of shape P onto shape Q

(b) rotation of shape Q onto shape R

(c) rotation of shape Q onto shape S

(d) rotation of shape S onto shape T

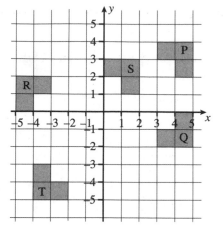

---

1 Copy this diagram.

(a) Translate triangle A 6 units left and 1 unit down. Label the new triangle B.

(b) Rotate triangle B 180° about (−3, 0). Label the new triangle C.

(c) Reflect triangle C in the *y*-axis. Label the new triangle D.

(d) Translate triangle D 1 unit down. Label the new triangle E.

(e) What single transformation will move triangle E onto triangle A?

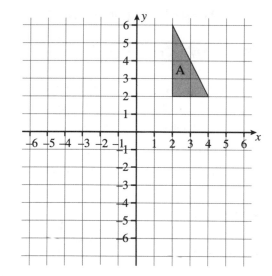

2 Copy this diagram.

(a) Rotate shape P 90° anticlockwise about (0, 0). Label the new shape Q.

(b) Reflect shape Q in the *y*-axis. Label the new shape R.

(c) Rotate shape R 90° anticlockwise about (1, −2). Label the new shape S.

(d) Reflect shape S in the *y*-axis. Label the new shape T.

(e) Describe the single translation which will move shape T onto shape P.

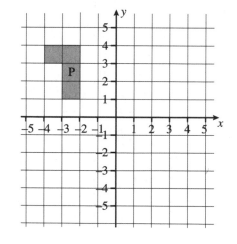

3

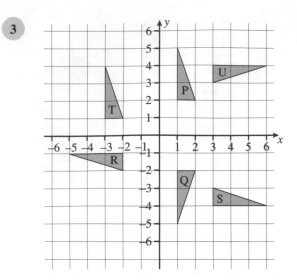

Describe fully the following transformations.

(a) triangle P onto triangle Q

(b) triangle Q onto triangle R

(c) triangle Q onto triangle S

(d) triangle P onto triangle T

(e) triangle P onto triangle U

(f) triangle S onto triangle U

4.3 Interpreting and sketching real–life graphs

HWK 1M/1E ———————————————————————————————— **Main Book Page 165**

1 The cost of making a telephone call depends on the duration of the call as shown below.

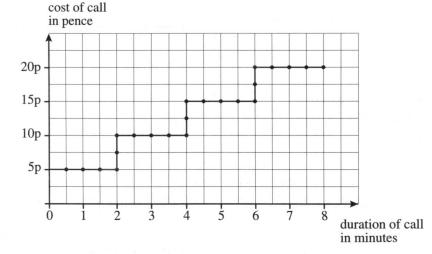

(a) How much is a call lasting
1 minute?

(b) How much is a call lasting
1 minute 30 seconds?

(c) How much is a call lasting
5 minutes?

(d) How much is a call lasting
6 minutes 30 seconds?

(e) How much is a call lasting 2 minutes
10 seconds?

(f) How much is a call lasting 4 minutes
27 seconds?

(g) What is the minimum charge for a call?

(h) A call costing 15p is between ____minutes
and _____ minutes in length. Fill in the
spaces.

2 Maggie has a peach tree. In the morning she picks a peach and places it on a window ledge in her kitchen. It is a very hot and sunny day.

In the evening she decides to put the peach in her freezer.

Sketch a graph to show the temperature of the peach during the day.

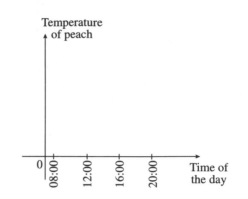

3 Distance from London

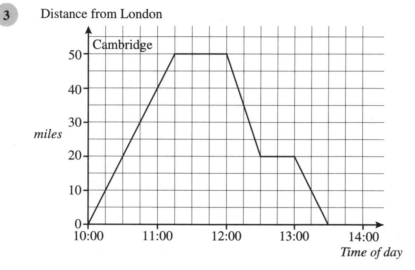

The graph above shows Alan's journey from London to Cambridge.

(a) When did he arrive at Cambridge?

(b) How long did he stop at Cambridge?

(c) When did he arrive back in London?

(d) Find Alan's speed on his journey from London to Cambridge.

(e) On his way back to London, Alan stops for half an hour. What is his speed for the final 20 miles of his journey?

4 A person jumps out of an aeroplane and freefalls before opening a parachute. He then glides to the ground. Sketch a graph to show how quickly he heads towards the ground.

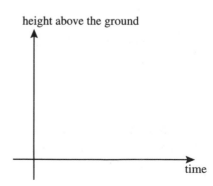

5   Draw a vertical axis on squared paper which goes up to 10 km. Draw a horizontal axis
    which goes up to 5 hours.

    Lucy leaves her house and walks for 1 hour at 4 km/h. She then stops at a shop for $\frac{1}{2}$ hour.
    She then walks at 6 km/h for $\frac{1}{2}$ hour.

    She now walks a further 1 km which takes her another $\frac{1}{2}$ hour. At this point she walks
    directly home at a speed of 4 km/h.

    Draw a travel graph to show Lucy's journey. When did she get back to her house?

4.4 Brackets and equations

HWK 1M ————————————————————————— **Main Book Page 171**

In questions ① to ⑥ answer true or false.

1   $3(x + 2) = 3x + 5$ 2 $5(x - 4) = 5x - 20$ 3 $2(4x + 3) = 14x$

4   $6(2x - 1) = 11x$ 5 $4(2x + 7) = 8x + 28$ 6 $3(2x - 1) = 6x - 3$

Expand (multiply out) the following expressions:

7    $6(x - 2)$ 8 $2(4x + 9)$ 9 $5(3x + 2)$

10   $x(m + n)$ 11 $y(a - b)$ 12 $m(n - 4)$

13   $p(m + 3)$ 14 $5(b + c)$ 15 $x(y - b)$

16   $a(b - c)$ 17 $x(3y + 2)$ 18 $a(a + 3)$

19   $x(x - 7)$ 20 $n(4 + n)$ 21 $4(2p - 1)$

22   Copy and complete

    (a) $4(3x - \square) = 12x - 8$ (b) $7(\square + 3p) = 42 + 21p$

    (c) $3(\square - \square) = 15a - 24$ (d) $\square(4 + \square) = 20 + 35n$

HWK 1E ————————————————————————— **Main Book Page 172**

In questions ① to ⑥ answer true or false.

1   $-4(x + 3) = -4x + 3$ 2 $-8(m - 2) = -8m - 16$

3   $-3(n + 2) = -3n - 6$ 4 $-9(a - 3) = -9a + 27$

5   $-5(2 - y) = -10 + 5y$ 6 $-2(4 + 3p) = -8 - 6p$

Expand (multiply out) the following expressions:

7 $-3(x + 6)$ **8** $-2(y - 3)$ **9** $-5(8 + m)$

10 $-4(6 - n)$ **11** $-5(2a - 1)$ **12** $-7(3 + 4p)$

13 $-2(2 + 7x)$ **14** $-6(4p - 5)$ **15** $-4(8 - 3m)$

16 $-9(1 - 4y)$ **17** $-10(6 + 5x)$ **18** $-3(9y - 2)$

HWK 2M — **Main Book Page 173**

Remove the brackets and simplify.

1 $4(x + 3) + 2(x + 5)$ **2** $5(x + 1) + 7(x + 3)$

3 $7(x + 4) + 6(x + 2)$ **4** $8(x + 3) + 4(x + 6)$

5 $6(2x + 3) + 2(x + 7)$ **6** $3(3x + 2) + 5(2x + 7)$

7 $4(3x + 1) + 3(5x + 2)$ **8** $7(4x + 2) + 2(8x + 3)$

9 $9(x + 3) + 5(4x + 5)$ **10** $6x + 3(2x + 1)$

11 $3 + 8(4x + 1)$ **12** $5(3x + 2) + 7x$

13 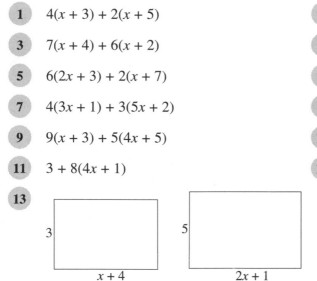 Write down an expression for the sum of the areas of these two rectangles. Simplify your answer.

3 and $x + 4$; 5 and $2x + 1$

14 Simplify $4(3x + 1) + 2(2x + 6) + 7(x + 8)$

15 Simplify $3(5x + 4) + 4(2 + 8x) + 8(2x + 5) + 2(1 + 7x)$

HWK 2E — **Main Book Page 174**

Remove the brackets and simplify.

1 $3(x + 4) + 2(x - 3)$ **2** $5(2x + 3) + 3(x - 2)$

3 $4(2x + 6) + 3(4x - 5)$ **4** $5(3x + 4) - 4(2x - 3)$

5 $6(2x - 1) + 5(3x + 2)$ **6** $7(2x + 3) - 5(x + 3)$

7 $8(4x + 7) - 4(3x + 8)$ **8** $6(5x + 9) - 2(10x - 1)$

68

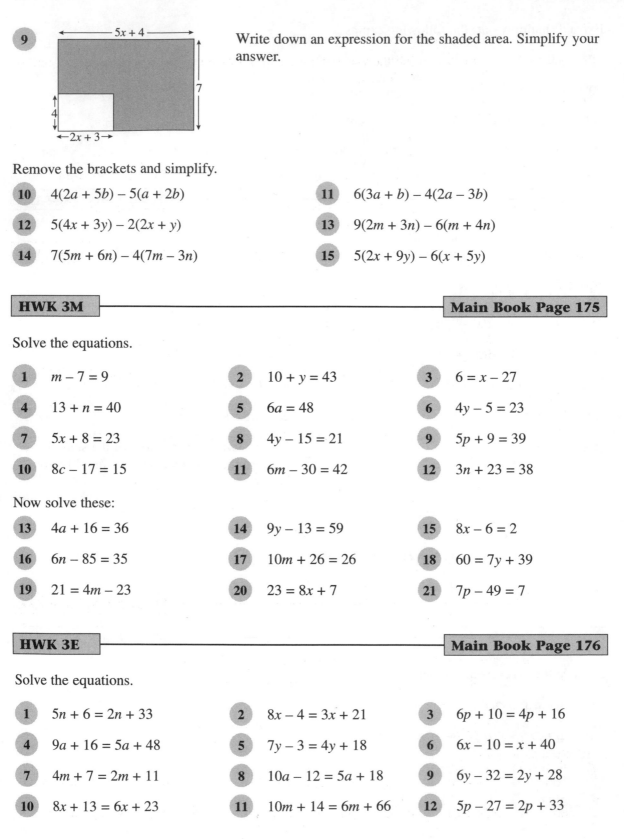

9 Write down an expression for the shaded area. Simplify your answer.

Remove the brackets and simplify.

10 $4(2a + 5b) - 5(a + 2b)$

11 $6(3a + b) - 4(2a - 3b)$

12 $5(4x + 3y) - 2(2x + y)$

13 $9(2m + 3n) - 6(m + 4n)$

14 $7(5m + 6n) - 4(7m - 3n)$

15 $5(2x + 9y) - 6(x + 5y)$

HWK 3M ———————————————————————————— **Main Book Page 175**

Solve the equations.

1 $m - 7 = 9$

2 $10 + y = 43$

3 $6 = x - 27$

4 $13 + n = 40$

5 $6a = 48$

6 $4y - 5 = 23$

7 $5x + 8 = 23$

8 $4y - 15 = 21$

9 $5p + 9 = 39$

10 $8c - 17 = 15$

11 $6m - 30 = 42$

12 $3n + 23 = 38$

Now solve these:

13 $4a + 16 = 36$

14 $9y - 13 = 59$

15 $8x - 6 = 2$

16 $6n - 85 = 35$

17 $10m + 26 = 26$

18 $60 = 7y + 39$

19 $21 = 4m - 23$

20 $23 = 8x + 7$

21 $7p - 49 = 7$

HWK 3E ———————————————————————————— **Main Book Page 176**

Solve the equations.

1 $5n + 6 = 2n + 33$

2 $8x - 4 = 3x + 21$

3 $6p + 10 = 4p + 16$

4 $9a + 16 = 5a + 48$

5 $7y - 3 = 4y + 18$

6 $6x - 10 = x + 40$

7 $4m + 7 = 2m + 11$

8 $10a - 12 = 5a + 18$

9 $6y - 32 = 2y + 28$

10 $8x + 13 = 6x + 23$

11 $10m + 14 = 6m + 66$

12 $5p - 27 = 2p + 33$

13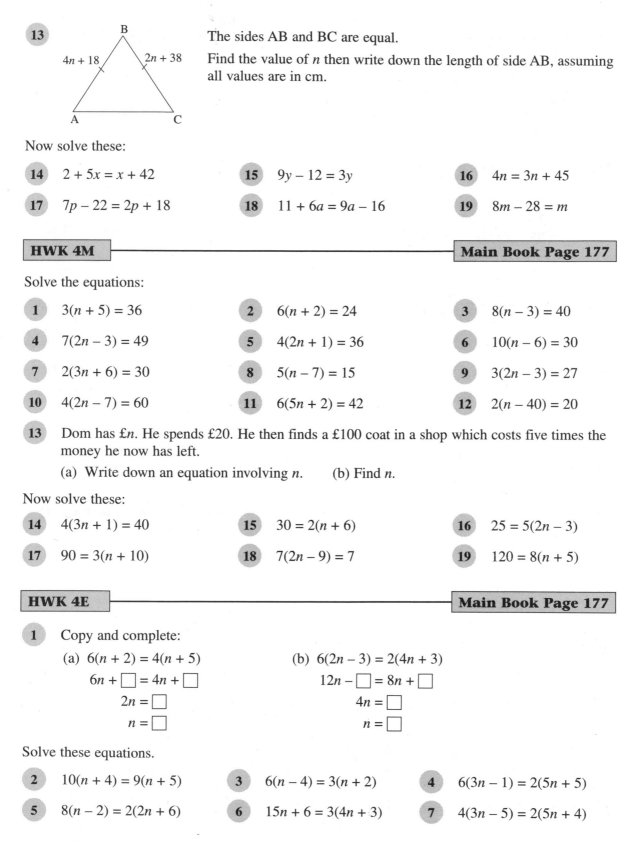

The sides AB and BC are equal.

Find the value of n then write down the length of side AB, assuming all values are in cm.

Now solve these:

14 $2 + 5x = x + 42$

15 $9y - 12 = 3y$

16 $4n = 3n + 45$

17 $7p - 22 = 2p + 18$

18 $11 + 6a = 9a - 16$

19 $8m - 28 = m$

HWK 4M ———————————————— **Main Book Page 177**

Solve the equations:

1 $3(n + 5) = 36$

2 $6(n + 2) = 24$

3 $8(n - 3) = 40$

4 $7(2n - 3) = 49$

5 $4(2n + 1) = 36$

6 $10(n - 6) = 30$

7 $2(3n + 6) = 30$

8 $5(n - 7) = 15$

9 $3(2n - 3) = 27$

10 $4(2n - 7) = 60$

11 $6(5n + 2) = 42$

12 $2(n - 40) = 20$

13 Dom has £n. He spends £20. He then finds a £100 coat in a shop which costs five times the money he now has left.

(a) Write down an equation involving n.   (b) Find n.

Now solve these:

14 $4(3n + 1) = 40$

15 $30 = 2(n + 6)$

16 $25 = 5(2n - 3)$

17 $90 = 3(n + 10)$

18 $7(2n - 9) = 7$

19 $120 = 8(n + 5)$

HWK 4E ———————————————— **Main Book Page 177**

1 Copy and complete:

(a) $6(n + 2) = 4(n + 5)$

$6n + \square = 4n + \square$

$2n = \square$

$n = \square$

(b) $6(2n - 3) = 2(4n + 3)$

$12n - \square = 8n + \square$

$4n = \square$

$n = \square$

Solve these equations.

2 $10(n + 4) = 9(n + 5)$

3 $6(n - 4) = 3(n + 2)$

4 $6(3n - 1) = 2(5n + 5)$

5 $8(n - 2) = 2(2n + 6)$

6 $15n + 6 = 3(4n + 3)$

7 $4(3n - 5) = 2(5n + 4)$

8 $7(n + 3) = 2(2n + 15)$ **9** $5(2n + 4) = 2(3n + 10)$ **10** $3(3n - 2) = 6n + 18$

11 $5(4n - 2) = 2(5n + 25)$

HWK 5M ───────────────────────────────────── **Main Book Page 178**

Use a calculator to find the answers to these questions by trying different numbers until you find the dimensions that give the required area.

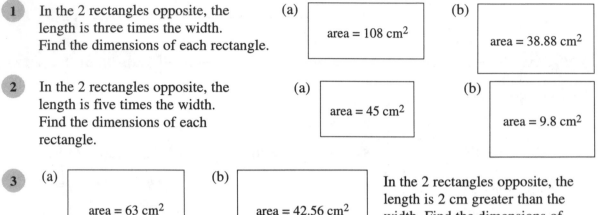

1 In the 2 rectangles opposite, the length is three times the width. Find the dimensions of each rectangle.

(a) area = 108 cm²

(b) area = 38.88 cm²

2 In the 2 rectangles opposite, the length is five times the width. Find the dimensions of each rectangle.

(a) area = 45 cm²

(b) area = 9.8 cm²

3 (a) area = 63 cm²

(b) area = 42.56 cm²

In the 2 rectangles opposite, the length is 2 cm greater than the width. Find the dimensions of each rectangle.

4 A rectangular room has an area of 26.24 m². Its length is 5 m greater than its width. Calculate the length of this room.

HWK 5E ───────────────────────────────────── **Main Book Page 179**

1

The area of this rectangle is 52 cm².

x

$x + 6$

Copy and complete this table to find x to one decimal place.

trial	calculation $x(x + 6)$	too large or too small?
$x = 5$	$5 \times 11 = ...$	too large
$x = 4$	$4 \times 10 = ...$	too small
$x = 4.8$	$4.8 \times 10.8 = ...$	too ...
$x = 4.9$	$4.9 \times 10.9 = ...$	too ...
so $x = ...$ cm to 1 decimal place.		

2 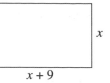 The area of this rectangle is 95 cm².

Copy and complete this table to find x to one decimal place.

trial	calculation $x(x + 9)$	too large or too small?
$x = 6$	$6 \times 15 = \ldots$	too small
$x = 7$	$7 \times 16 = \ldots$	too large
$x = 6.5$	$6.5 \times 15.5 = \ldots$	too ...
$x = 6.4$	$6.4 \times 15.4 = \ldots$	too ...
$x = 6.2$	$6.2 \times 15.2 = \ldots$	too ...
$x = 6.3$	$6.3 \times 15.3 = \ldots$	too ...
so $x = \ldots$ cm to 1 decimal place.		

3 Use trial and improvement for each rectangle below to find the value of x to 1 decimal place. Make a table like questions **1** and **2**.

(a) area = 100 cm², x, $x + 3$ (b) area = 147 cm², x, $x + 7$

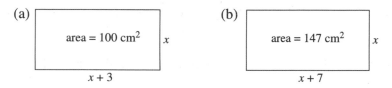

HWK 6M/6E ——————————————— **Main Book Page 181**

In questions **1** to **5** form an equation and then solve it to find the number.

1 If we multiply the number by 4 and then subtract 6, the answer is 50.

2 If we double the number and add 15, the answer is 53.

3 If we add 7 to the number and then double the result, the answer is 58.

4 If we subtract 15 from the number and then multiply the result by 3, the answer is 48.

5 If we subtract 14 from the number and then multiply the result by 6, the answer is 66.

6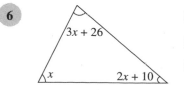

(a) Form an equation involving x.

(b) Solve the equation to find x.

(c) Write down the value of each angle in the triangle.

7

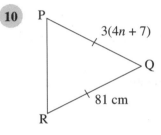

$x + 2$

$3x + 1$

The perimeter of this rectangle is 38 cm.

(a) Form an equation involving x.

(b) Solve the equation to find x.

(c) Write down the values of the length and width of the rectangle.

8 Alex has £$(6n + 3)$ and Fiona has £$(3n + 15)$. If they both have the same amount of money, form an equation involving n. Solve the equation and write down how much money Fiona has.

9 This rectangle has an area of 120 cm².
Form an equation and solve it to find x.

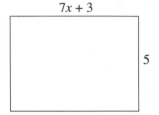

$7x + 3$

5

10

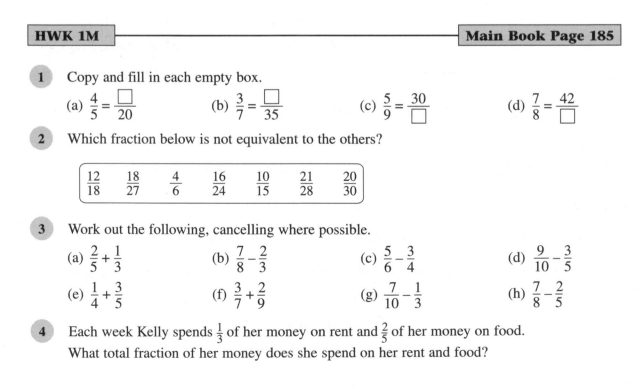

P

$3(4n + 7)$

Q

81 cm

R

PQ and QR are the equal sides in an isosceles triangle.
Find the value of n.

4.5 Fractions review

HWK 1M ———————————————— **Main Book Page 185**

1 Copy and fill in each empty box.

(a) $\frac{4}{5} = \frac{\square}{20}$

(b) $\frac{3}{7} = \frac{\square}{35}$

(c) $\frac{5}{9} = \frac{30}{\square}$

(d) $\frac{7}{8} = \frac{42}{\square}$

2 Which fraction below is not equivalent to the others?

$$\frac{12}{18} \quad \frac{18}{27} \quad \frac{4}{6} \quad \frac{16}{24} \quad \frac{10}{15} \quad \frac{21}{28} \quad \frac{20}{30}$$

3 Work out the following, cancelling where possible.

(a) $\frac{2}{5} + \frac{1}{3}$

(b) $\frac{7}{8} - \frac{2}{3}$

(c) $\frac{5}{6} - \frac{3}{4}$

(d) $\frac{9}{10} - \frac{3}{5}$

(e) $\frac{1}{4} + \frac{3}{5}$

(f) $\frac{3}{7} + \frac{2}{9}$

(g) $\frac{7}{10} - \frac{1}{3}$

(h) $\frac{7}{8} - \frac{2}{5}$

4 Each week Kelly spends $\frac{1}{3}$ of her money on rent and $\frac{2}{5}$ of her money on food.
What total fraction of her money does she spend on her rent and food?

HWK 1E ──────────────────────────────── **Main Book Page 186**

1. $\frac{4}{7}$ of a garden is covered by a lawn and $\frac{1}{3}$ is paved. What fraction of the garden is *not* a lawn and *not* paved?

2. Work out, leaving each answer as a mixed number.

   (a) $1\frac{1}{3} + \frac{1}{4}$ (b) $2\frac{1}{2} - \frac{3}{5}$ (c) $3\frac{1}{4} - 1\frac{1}{3}$

   (d) $2\frac{1}{4} + 1\frac{1}{10}$ (e) $1\frac{2}{3} + 3\frac{1}{2}$ (f) $3\frac{1}{3} - 2\frac{1}{2}$

   (g) $2\frac{3}{4} - 1\frac{2}{3}$ (h) $1\frac{7}{10} + 1\frac{1}{4}$ (i) $3\frac{3}{4} + 1\frac{2}{5}$

3. Robyn weighs $8\frac{3}{4}$ stones and Nathan weighs $8\frac{4}{7}$ stones. How much heavier is Robyn than Nathan?

4. 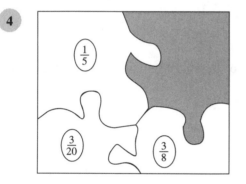 The fractions show what proportion of this jigsaw each piece covers. What fraction of the jigsaw is covered by the shaded piece?

HWK 2M ──────────────────────────────── **Main Book Page 187**

1. Which answer is the odd one out?

   $\frac{5}{6}$ of 12 $\frac{2}{3}$ of 18 $\frac{3}{5}$ of 20

2. Janet has £96. She spends $\frac{5}{8}$ of her money on a jacket. How much money does she have left?

3. Work out

   (a) $\frac{5}{9}$ of 72   (b) $\frac{3}{7}$ of 42   (c) $\frac{7}{10}$ of 50   (d) $\frac{2}{5}$ of 60

4. A shop increases all its prices by $\frac{2}{9}$. Write down the new cost of each item shown below.

trousers	shirt	coat
£36	£27	£108

5 Toni runs for $\frac{7}{12}$ of 4 hours. How many minutes does she run for?

6 Hans needs to use $\frac{9}{25}$ of his flour to bake. If he has 2 kg of flour to start with, how much flour will he have left after baking?

7 Decrease 72 by $\frac{5}{6}$.

HWK 2E ──────────────────────────────── **Main Book Page 187**

1 Work out, cancelling when possible.

(a) $\frac{5}{6} \times \frac{1}{4}$ (b) $\frac{3}{7} \times \frac{2}{5}$ (c) $\frac{5}{8} \times \frac{3}{4}$ (d) $\frac{4}{9} \times \frac{3}{7}$

(e) $\frac{3}{8} \times \frac{5}{6}$ (f) $\frac{2}{7} \times \frac{3}{4}$ (g) $\frac{6}{7} \times \frac{2}{3}$ (h) $\frac{3}{5} \times \frac{5}{6}$

(i) $\frac{4}{9} \times \frac{18}{1}$ (j) $\frac{5}{6} \times 24$ (k) $\frac{9}{10} \times 30$ (l) $\frac{3}{8} \times 4$

2 Ben is running a $3\frac{1}{2}$ km race. He leads for the first $\frac{4}{7}$ of the race. How many km is this?

3

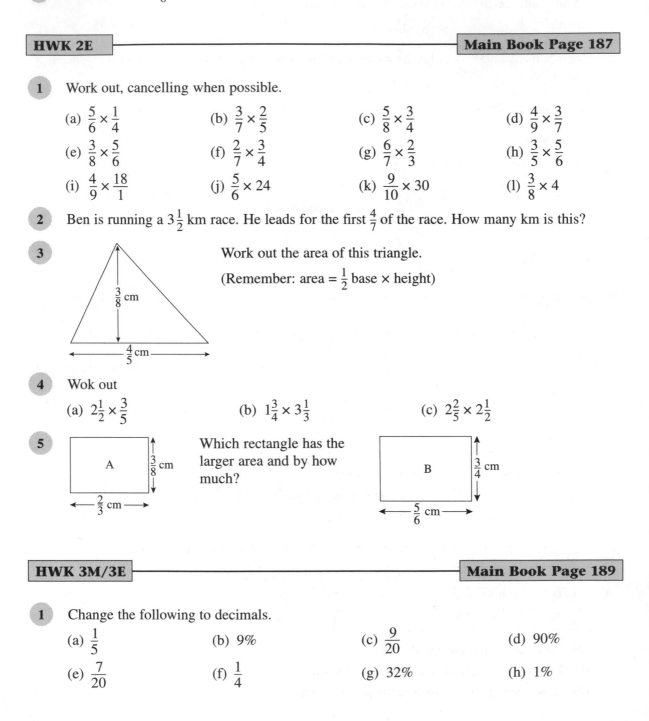

Work out the area of this triangle.

(Remember: area = $\frac{1}{2}$ base $\times$ height)

$\frac{3}{8}$ cm

$\frac{4}{5}$ cm

4 Wok out

(a) $2\frac{1}{2} \times \frac{3}{5}$ (b) $1\frac{3}{4} \times 3\frac{1}{3}$ (c) $2\frac{2}{5} \times 2\frac{1}{2}$

5

A $\frac{3}{8}$ cm

$\frac{2}{3}$ cm

Which rectangle has the larger area and by how much?

B $\frac{3}{4}$ cm

$\frac{5}{6}$ cm

HWK 3M/3E ──────────────────────────────── **Main Book Page 189**

1 Change the following to decimals.

(a) $\frac{1}{5}$ (b) 9%   (c) $\frac{9}{20}$ (d) 90%

(e) $\frac{7}{20}$ (f) $\frac{1}{4}$ (g) 32%   (h) 1%

2 Which is larger? $\dfrac{13}{20}$ or 62%

3 Carl spends 0.7 of his money. What fraction of his money does he have left?

4 Change the following to percentages.

(a) 0.4   (b) $\dfrac{3}{25}$ (c) $\dfrac{3}{4}$ (d) 0.03

5 Wendy has painted $\dfrac{11}{20}$ of her living room. What percentage of her living room is not painted?

6 Change the following to fractions, cancelling when possible.

(a) 0.02   (b) 7%   (c) 0.84   (d) 32%

7 Write in order of size, largest first.

0.3   29% $\dfrac{1}{4}$ 0.32 $\dfrac{7}{25}$

4.6 Handling data

HWK 1M   **Main Book Page 190**

1 The table below shows the expected crowd size, cost of a ticket and number of goals expected at the next match for 3 football teams.

team	crowd size	ticket cost (£)	number of goals
Chelsea	43000	52	2
Manchester United	72000	60	3
Aston Villa	54000	45	2

(a) Which team has the highest ticket cost?

(b) Which team expects the highest number of goals in the next match?

(c) Which team will have the lowest crowd size?

2 The hair colour of children in a primary school is recorded in the table below.

	dark hair	blond hair	other colours
boys	43	39	16
girls	32	51	19

(a) How many girls have dark hair?

(b) How many children in total have blond hair?

(c) How many girls are there in the primary school?

3

name	weekly hours in July	weekly hours in January
Mark	84	28
Amy	73	21
Gwyn	79	40
Tasha	72	14

Mark, Amy, Gwyn and Tasha work in restaurants in a seaside town.

The table shows the number of hours they work each week in July and January.

(a) Who worked the most weekly hours in July?

(b) How many hours more did Tasha work each week in July than January?

(c) How many hours less than Gwyn did Amy work each week in July?

4 The table opposite shows the cost per mile if a petrol or diesel car is used.

The next table shows the road distances in miles between various cities.

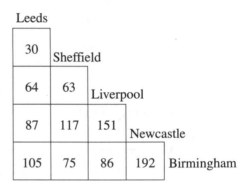

petrol	12.5p per mile
diesel	8p per mile

(a) Ugo drives a petrol car from Liverpool to Birmingham. How much money does he spend on the petrol?

(b) Chloe drives a diesel car from Leeds to Newcastle. How much money does she spend on diesel?

(c) Ugo now drives from Birmingham to Sheffield to Newcastle then back to Birmingham again. How much money does he spend on petrol for this complete round trip?

HWK 1E ———————————————————————————— **Main Book Page 192**

1 The heights of two groups of teenagers are measured. The heights for each group are shown in the frequency diagrams below.

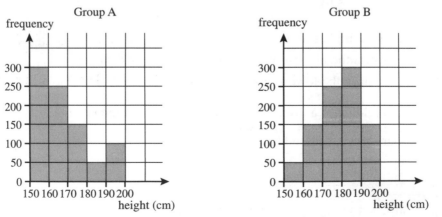

(a) Which group of teenagers is generally taller?

(b) Which frequency diagram would you expect if you measured the heights of all the teenagers in a Sixth Form College? Explain your answer.

2 (a) 18 ten-year-old children run a 400 metre race. Their times t (in seconds) are shown below.

64, 63, 86, 75, 81, 92, 74, 77, 85,

93, 76, 65, 84, 91, 73, 83, 76, 75

Put the heights into groups.

class interval	frequency
$60 \leq t < 70$	
$70 \leq t < 80$	
$80 \leq t < 90$	
$90 \leq t < 100$	

(b) Draw a frequency diagram like those in question **1**.

frequency

time (seconds)

60 70 80 90 100

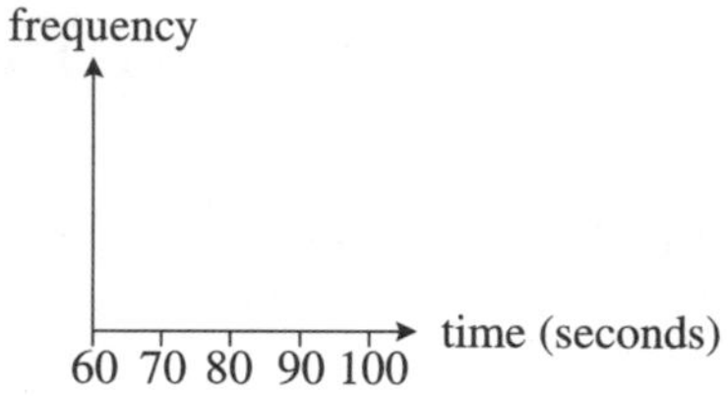

(c) The same children run a 400 metre race when they are seventeen years old.
Their times t (in seconds) are shown below.

67, 56, 65, 57, 53, 74, 59, 53, 71

68, 52, 66, 75, 61, 54, 62, 56, 63

Put the heights into groups similar to part (a).

(d) Draw a frequency diagram like those in question (1).

(e) Write a sentence to compare the times shown by each frequency diagram.
Suggest a reason for the difference.

HWK 2M ———————————————————— **Main Book Page 194**

1 72 people were asked what their favourite type of chocolate was. The results are shown in the table below.

type of chocolate	frequency
milk	32
dark	30
white	10

(a) Work out the angle on a pie chart for one person (ie. $360° \div$ total number of people).

(b) Work out the angle for each type of chocolate and draw a pie chart.

78

In questions ②, ③ and ④ work out the angle for each sector and draw a pie chart.

② Favourite type of music.

type of music	frequency
rock	14
jazz	6
soul	7
classical	9
dance	4

③ Favourite European Capital City

Capital City	frequency
Paris	6
Rome	6
London	8
Berlin	1
Madrid	3

② Favourite ice-cream flavour

ice-cream	frequency
strawberry	136
vanilla	100
chocolate	240
neopolitan	120
mint	52
ginger	72

HWK 2E ——————————————————— **Main Book Page 194**

1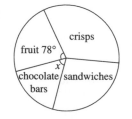
Year 8 children who bring packed lunches to school are asked what main items they have in their lunch. The pie chart opposite shows the results.

40% of items are crisps and $\frac{1}{4}$ are sandwiches.

Calculate the size of angle x in the pie chart.

2 A garage records the type of vehicle stopping for petrol one day. The results are shown in the table below.

type of vehicle	percentage
car	50%
van	20%
motorbike	15%
lorry	10%
other	5%

Find the angle on a pie chart for each type of vehicle then draw the pie chart.

3 900 pupils in Cork Field School and 350 pupils in Manor High School were asked what they enjoyed doing most at weekends. The results are shown in the two pie charts.

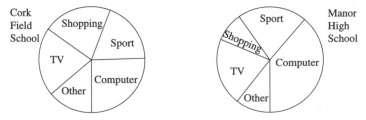

Did more pupils in Manor High School choose using the computer than pupils in Cork Field School or less? *Explain* your answer.

1 The scatter graph shows the waist sizes and weights of some people.

   (a) How many people weighed more than 70 kg?

   (b) How many people had a waist size of less than 36 inches?

   (c) Answer *true* or *false*: 'In general as waist size increases, weight increases.'

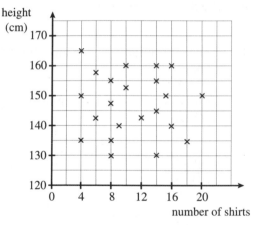

2 The scatter graph shows the heights of some people and how many shirts they own.

   (a) How many people are more than 150 cm tall?

   (b) How many people own less than 8 shirts?

   (c) Answer *true* or *false*: 'In general as the number of shirts increases, height increases.'

3

french test	german test
13	14
19	17
16	17
8	8
16	15
3	4
10	11
20	19
18	18
7	5
11	12
18	19
10	8
12	10
9	9
15	16

The table shows two test scores obtained by 16 children in year 8 for french and german.

(a) Draw the axes shown below and complete the scatter graph.

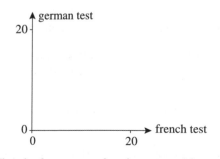

(b) What is the connection in general between the french and german test marks?

80

UNIT 5

5.1 Ratio and Proportion

HWK 1M ──────────────────────────── Main Book Page 210HWK 1M ──────────────────────────── Main Book Page 210

1 30:18 is the same as 5:3 because both numbers can be divided by 6.
   Write these ratios in a more simple form.

   (a) 32:12 (b) 20:120 (c) 15:40 (d) 12:18:36

   (e) 21:35 (f) 54:36 (g) 28:16:32 (h) 18:45:27

2 There are 90 boys and 70 girls on the school field. Write down the ratio of boys to girls in its simplest form.

3 The Carlton family have three times as many rabbits as dogs. Write down the ratio of rabbits to dogs.

4 The ratio of men to women in a drama group is 5:3. If there are 20 men, how many women are there?

5   Write down the ratio of noughts to crosses in its simplest form.

6 Charlie has cartons of juice in a large box. The ratio of orange to apple is 3:4. If Charlie has 18 cartons of orange juice, how many cartons of apple juice does he have?

7 Toni has some felt tip pens. The colours red to blue to green are in the ratio 5:2:3. If Toni has 12 green pens, how many red pens does she have and how many blue pens does she have?

8 Margaret and Kelly go out on their bikes one day. The ratio of the distances they travel is 7:12. Kelly travels the furthest. If Kelly travels 36 km, how far does Margaret travel?

HWK 1E ──────────────────────────── Main Book Page 212HWK 1E ──────────────────────────── Main Book Page 212

1 Nick and Beth share a bag of 32 toffees in the ratio 3:5. How many toffees does each person get?

2 Some red and blue paint is mixed together in the ratio 7:2. If 27 litres of paint is used in total, how much of each colour paint is used?

3 Share each quantity in the ratio given.

(a) £800, 3:7   (b) £144, 7:5   (c) £1500, 3:1:6

4 In Jennifer's workshop, the ratio of nails to screws is 9:5. If there are 450 screws, how many nails are there?

5 The angles in a triangle are in the ratio 4:3:2. Find the size of the largest angle.

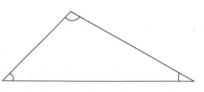

6 Find the smallest share in each of these problems.

(a) £48, ratio 5:11   (b) 320 kg, ratio 5:2:3

7 The marks in an exam are given for three different parts in the ratio 11:5:4. The maximum mark for the exam is 100. Write down the maximum marks which can be awarded for each part of the exam.

8 Hugo and Ellie's mother gives them £80 in the ratio 7:9. Hugo gets the smaller share. Hugo owes Ellie £15 and so he gives her this money.

Write down the ratio of Hugo's money to Ellie's money now. Write the ratio in its simplest form.

9

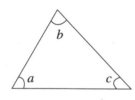

Angles in the triangle above are in the ratio 5:4:3.
Angle *b* is the middle sized angle.

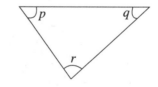

Angles in the triangle above are in the ratio 3:1:5. Angle *p* is the middle sized angle. Angle *r* is the largest angle.

Find the size of angle *r* if angle *p* is equal in size to angle *b*.

HWK 2M   **Main Book Page 213**

You may use a calculator.

1 Find the cost of 9 bars of chocolate if 5 bars of chocolate cost £3.90.

2 If 4 plates cost £28.80, find the cost of 11 plates.

3 3 footballs cost £25.35. Find the cost of 7 footballs.

4 6 boxes of cereal weigh 3480 g. How much will 15 boxes of cereal weigh?

5 Mitchell's heart beats 325 times in 5 minutes. How many times will his heart beat in 4 minutes?

6 Fiona takes 42 minutes to travels 49 miles on a motorway. If she drives at the same speed, how long will it take her to travel 84 miles?

7

£25 can be exchanged for $36.25
£40 can be exchanged for 44 euros

Use the information above to:

(a) change £40 into dollars

(b) change £25 into euros

(c) Mark buys a meal for $31.90 and Sophie buys a meal for 26.4 euros. Who had the most expensive meal and by how many pounds more expensive was it?

8 Ronnie can buy an Easter egg for £2.99 each or he can buy six Easter eggs for £15. How much money per egg will Ronnie save if he chooses the six egg deal?

9 Sureway supermarket sells 12 chocolate eclairs for £4.08. Dan's deli sells 8 chocolate eclairs for £2.56. Which shop offers the cheaper chocolate eclair and by how much is it cheaper?

HWK 2E ——————————————————————————— **Main Book Page 215**

1 The scale of a map is 1:100 000. The distance between 2 towns is 8 cm. What is the actual distance in kilometres between the two towns?

2 Find the actual distance in metres between two pylons which are 2 cm apart on a map whose scale is 1:10 000.

3 The length of a field on a map is 1.5 cm. Find the actual length of the field if the map scale is 1:40 000.

4 Two cities are 6.5 cm apart on a map and the scale of the map is 1:2 000 000. What is the actual distance between the two cities?

5 A map has a scale of 1:50 000. The distance from Tom's house to the 'Red Bull' pub is 3 cm and the distance from Tom's house to the 'White Horse' pub is 5.5 cm. How many kilometres further from Tom's house is the White Horse than the Red Bull?

6 Colin and Adele are hiking. They fix their positions and are 12 km from each other. How far is this on a map if the scale is 1:200 000?

7 Two ships are 30 km apart from each other. How far is this on a map if the scale is 1:50 000?

8 Map A has a scale of 1:200 000. Map B has a scale of 1:50 000. Two villages are 8 cm apart on map A. How far apart will the two villages be on map B?

5.2 Negative numbers review

HWK 1M ──────────────────────────── **Main Book Page 216**

1 Work out

(a) $3 + (-5)$ (b) $3 - 5$ (c) $-3 - 5$ (d) $-6 + 2$

(e) $-1 + (-3)$ (f) $5 - (-2)$ (g) $-3 - (-2)$ (h) $4 + (-6)$

2 Answer true or false.

(a) $-4 + 2 = -6$ (b) $-5 - 1 = -4$ (c) $7 + (-4) = 3$

(d) $-1 - (-3) = 2$ (e) $-4 + (-2) = -2$ (f) $-3 - 6 = -9$

3 Six judges in a dance competition give the following scores:

| +3 | | −1 | | −2 | | +1 | | +5 | | −2 |

What is the total score given by these judges?

4 Copy and fill in the empty boxes below:

(a) $-2 + \boxed{} = 1$ (b) $-5 - \boxed{} = -1$ (c) $\boxed{} + (-2) = -6$

(d) $-3 - \boxed{} = -7$ (e) $\boxed{} + (-3) = -4$ (f) $-7 - \boxed{} = -5$

5 What is the value of m if $m + m + m = -12$?

6 Work out

(a) $-6 + (-2) - (-4)$ (b) $-9 - (-7) - 2$ (c) $-3 - (-4) - (-1) - 6 + (-4)$

(d) $-5 - 2 + (-3) - (-6) - 2$ (e) $1 + (-4) - (-2) - 4 + (-3) - (-6)$

HWK 1E ──────────────────────────── **Main Book Page 217**

1 Work out

(a) $3 \times (-6)$ (b) $-2 \times (-4)$ (c) -3×5 (d) $-8 \times (-4)$

(e) $12 \div (-4)$ (f) $-20 \div (-4)$ (g) $-30 \div 6$ (h) -7×6

(i) $-35 \div (-5)$

2 Find the value of mn if $m = -4$ and $n = -6$.

3 Find the value of p^2 if $p = -3$.

4 Copy and complete each number chain.

(a)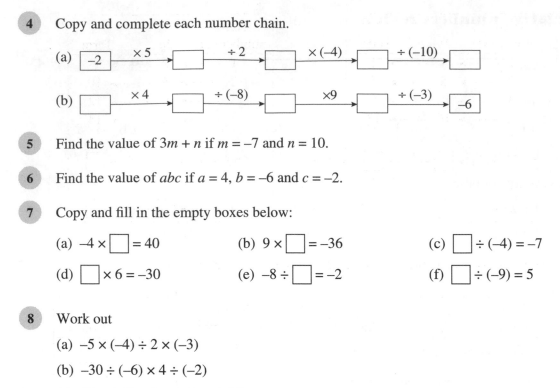

$\boxed{-2} \xrightarrow{\times 5} \boxed{} \xrightarrow{\div 2} \boxed{} \xrightarrow{\times (-4)} \boxed{} \xrightarrow{\div (-10)} \boxed{}$

(b) $\boxed{} \xrightarrow{\times 4} \boxed{} \xrightarrow{\div (-8)} \boxed{} \xrightarrow{\times 9} \boxed{} \xrightarrow{\div (-3)} \boxed{-6}$

5 Find the value of $3m + n$ if $m = -7$ and $n = 10$.

6 Find the value of abc if $a = 4$, $b = -6$ and $c = -2$.

7 Copy and fill in the empty boxes below:

(a) $-4 \times \boxed{} = 40$ (b) $9 \times \boxed{} = -36$ (c) $\boxed{} \div (-4) = -7$

(d) $\boxed{} \times 6 = -30$ (e) $-8 \div \boxed{} = -2$ (f) $\boxed{} \div (-9) = 5$

8 Work out

(a) $-5 \times (-4) \div 2 \times (-3)$

(b) $-30 \div (-6) \times 4 \div (-2)$

(c) $50 \div (-5) \div 2 \times (-8) \div (-10)$

5.3 Sequences – the *n*th term

HWK 1M   **Main Book Page 219**

1 Copy and complete these mapping diagrams for finding sequences rules.

(a)

Term number (n)	$3n$	Term
1 →	3 →	5
2 →	6 →	8
3 →	9 →	11
4 →	12 →	14
⋮	⋮	⋮
10 →	□ →	□
⋮	⋮	⋮
n →	$3n$ →	$3n + 2$

(b)

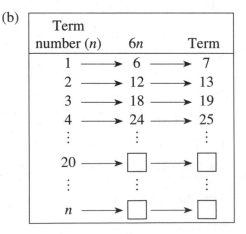

Term number (n)	$6n$	Term
1 →	6 →	7
2 →	12 →	13
3 →	18 →	19
4 →	24 →	25
⋮	⋮	⋮
20 →	□ →	□
⋮	⋮	⋮
n →	□ →	□

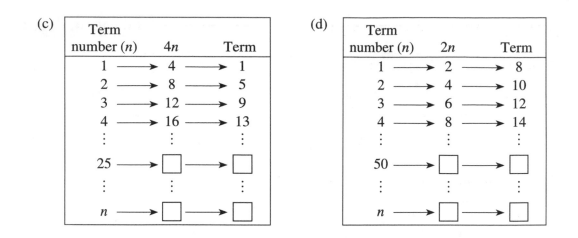

2 Here you are given the *n*th term. Copy and complete the diagrams.

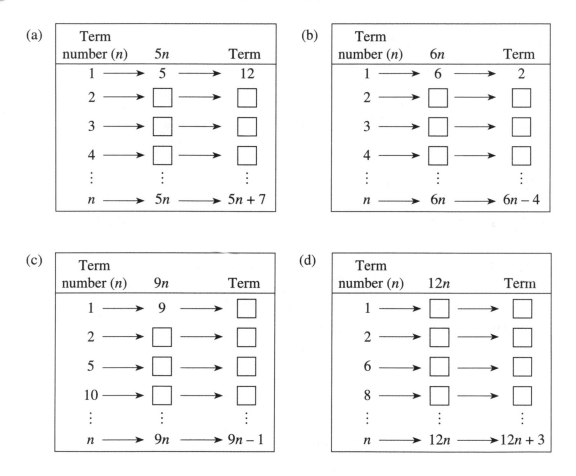

1 $4n - 1$ $n + 4$ $2n$ $n - 1$ $3n + 2$ $4n$

Write down each sequence below and match it to the correct expression for the nth term shown above.

(a) 4, 8, 12, 16, …

(b) 3, 7, 11, 15, …

(c) 0, 1, 2, 3, 4, …

(d) 5, 8, 11, 14, 17, …

2   Callum is on the beach collecting shells.

After 1 hour he has collected 15 shells.

After 2 hours he has 25 shells.

After 3 hours he has 35 shells.

After 4 hours he has 45 shells.

(a) How many shells do you expect him to have after 5 hours?

(b) Answer true or false. 'After n hours he will have $(15n + 10)$ shells.'

3   One fence panel has 4 vertical strips of wood.

Two fence panels joined together as shown have
7 vertical strips.

Three fence panels joined together are shown.

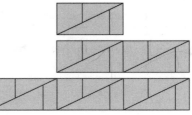

(a) How many vertical strips do 3 fence panels have?

(b) Draw four fence panels joined together.

(c) How many vertical strips do 4 fence panels have?

(d) How many vertical strips do 5 fence panels have?

(e) Copy and fill in the empty box:

'The number of vertical strips for n fence panels is $3n + \boxed{}$'

4   Copy and complete:

(a) 8, 11, 14, 17, … nth term $= 3n + \boxed{}$

(b) 11, 13, 15, 17, … nth term $= 2n + \boxed{}$

(c) 1, 6, 11, 16, …. nth term $= 5n - \boxed{}$

(d) 3, 13, 23, 33, … nth term $= 10n - \boxed{}$

HWK 2M ──────────────────────────────── **Main Book Page 222**

1 Look at the sequence 5, 8, 11, 14, …
The *difference* between terms is 3.
Copy the table which has a column for $3n$.
Copy and complete:
'The nth term of the sequence is $3n +$ ☐ .'

n	$3n$	term
1	3	5
2	6	8
3	9	11
4	12	14

2 Look at each sequence and the table underneath.
Find the nth term in each case.

(a) Sequence 8, 13, 18, 23, …

n	$5n$	term
1	5	8
2	10	13
3	☐	18
4	☐	23

nth term = ☐

(b) Sequence 2, 6, 10, 14, …

n	$4n$	term
1	4	2
2	☐	6
3	☐	10
4	☐	14

nth term = ☐

3 Look at the sequence 5, 7, 9, 11, …
Write down the *difference* between terms.
Make a table like those in question **2** and use it to find the nth term.

4 Write down each sequence in a table and then find the nth term.
(a) 2, 8, 14, 20, …
(b) 10, 13, 16, 19, …
(c) 13, 22, 31, 40, …
(d) 7, 17, 27, 37, …
(e) 1, 6, 11, 16, …

HWK 2E ──────────────────────────────── **Main Book Page 223**

In these questions you are given a sequence of shapes made from sticks or dots.
If you need to, make a table to help you find the nth term of the sequence.

1 A pattern of sticks is made as shown below.

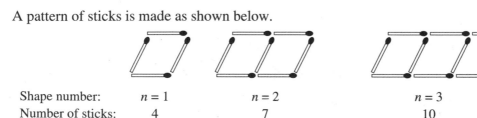

Shape number:	$n = 1$	$n = 2$	$n = 3$
Number of sticks:	4	7	10

Draw shape number 4 and shape number 5. How many sticks are there in the nth term?

2   Here is a pattern made with dots.

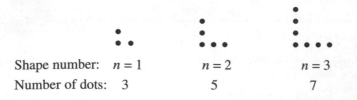

Shape number: $n = 1$ $n = 2$ $n = 3$
Number of dots: 3   5   7

Draw the next diagram in the sequence. How many dots are there in the nth term?

3   Here is another pattern made with dots.

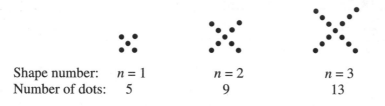

Shape number: $n = 1$ $n = 2$ $n = 3$
Number of dots: 5   9   13

Draw the next diagram in the sequence. How many dots are there in the nth term?

4   Here is a sequence of hexagons made from sticks.

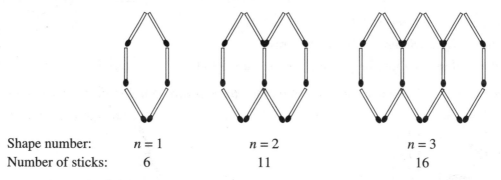

Shape number: $n = 1$ $n = 2$ $n = 3$
Number of sticks: 6   11   16

Draw shape number 4. How many sticks are there in the nth term?

5   Here is another pattern made with dots.

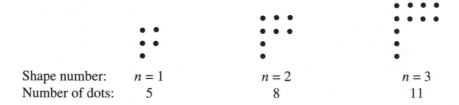

Shape number: $n = 1$ $n = 2$ $n = 3$
Number of dots: 5   8   11

Draw the next diagram in the sequence. How many dots are there in the nth term?

5.4 Enlargement

Enlarge the shapes in questions **1** to **6** by the scale factor given. Make sure you leave room on your page for the enlargement.

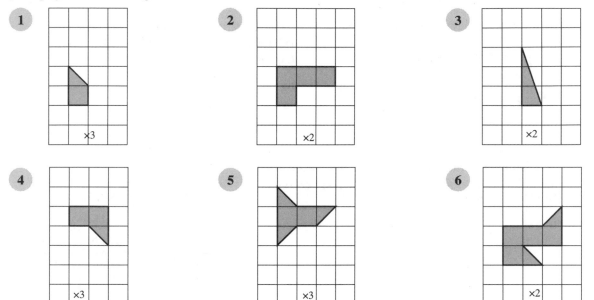

In questions **7** to **10**, look at each pair of diagrams and decide whether or not one diagram is an enlargement of the other. For each question write the scale factor of the enlargement or write 'not an enlargement'.

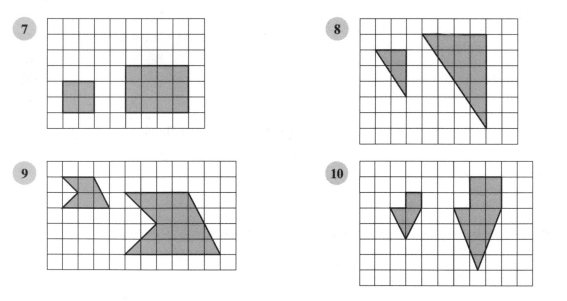

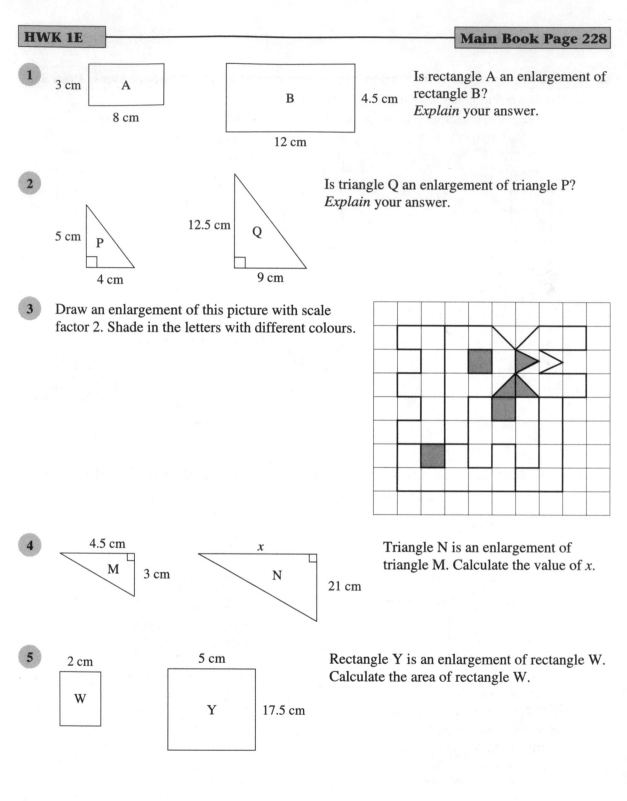

1   3 cm   A   8 cm

B   4.5 cm   12 cm

Is rectangle A an enlargement of rectangle B?
Explain your answer.

2

5 cm   P   4 cm

12.5 cm   Q   9 cm

Is triangle Q an enlargement of triangle P?
Explain your answer.

3   Draw an enlargement of this picture with scale factor 2. Shade in the letters with different colours.

4   4.5 cm   M   3 cm

x   N   21 cm

Triangle N is an enlargement of triangle M. Calculate the value of *x*.

5   2 cm   W

5 cm   Y   17.5 cm

Rectangle Y is an enlargement of rectangle W. Calculate the area of rectangle W.

In questions ① to ⑥ copy the diagram and then draw an enlargement using the scale factor and centre of enlargement given. Leave room for the enlargement.

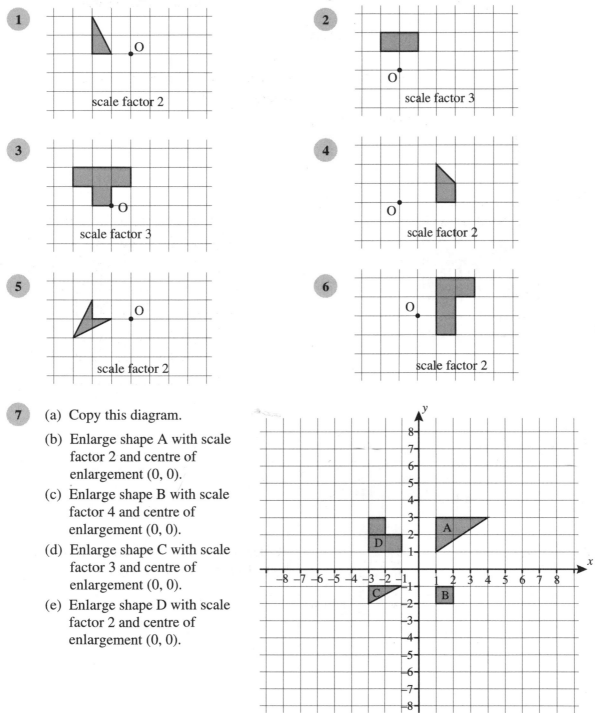

① scale factor 2

② scale factor 3

③ scale factor 3

④ scale factor 2

⑤ scale factor 2

⑥ scale factor 2

⑦ (a) Copy this diagram.

(b) Enlarge shape A with scale factor 2 and centre of enlargement (0, 0).

(c) Enlarge shape B with scale factor 4 and centre of enlargement (0, 0).

(d) Enlarge shape C with scale factor 3 and centre of enlargement (0, 0).

(e) Enlarge shape D with scale factor 2 and centre of enlargement (0, 0).

Draw the shapes and then draw lines through corresponding points to find the centre of enlargement. Do not draw the shapes too near the edge of the page!

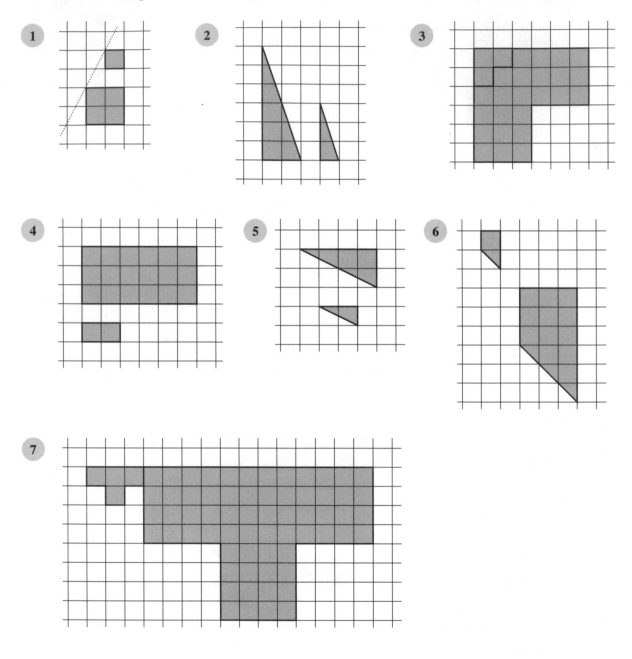

5.5 Congruent shapes, tessellation

1 Decide which shapes are congruent pairs. (You can use tracing paper)

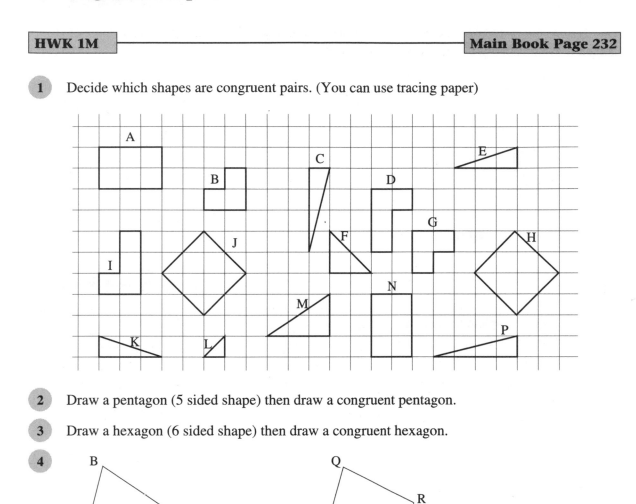

2 Draw a pentagon (5 sided shape) then draw a congruent pentagon.

3 Draw a hexagon (6 sided shape) then draw a congruent hexagon.

4

The two shapes above are congruent. Sam says that side AD is equal to side SR. Is Sam correct?

5 Draw and colour a design which uses at least 3 different types of congruent shape.

1. Draw any quadrilateral (4 sided shape) on paper or card and cut it out. Use this template to draw a tessellation and colour in this pattern.

2. Draw another tessellation pattern using at least two different shapes. Colour in this pattern. An example is shown opposite.

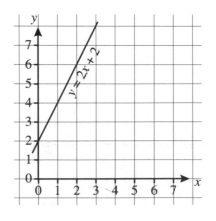

5.6 Drawing graphs review

1. Copy and complete the table for $y = 2x + 1$

x	0	1	2	3	4	5
y				7		
coordinates				(3, 7)		

   Draw the graph of $y = 2x + 1$ using 2 cm for 1 unit on the x-axis and 1 cm for 1 unit on the y-axis.

2. Copy and complete the table for $y = 6 - x$

x	0	1	2	3	4	5	6
y			4				
coordinates			(2, 4)				

   Draw the graph of $y = 6 - x$ using 1 cm for 1 unit on the x-axis and the y-axis.

3. Use a table of values to draw $y = x^2 + 1$ for x-values from -3 to 3.

4. (a) Copy this diagram showing the line $y = 2x + 2$.

   (b) Draw the line $y = 5$.

   (c) Draw the line $x = 2$.

   (d) Write down the co-ordinates of the point where the line $x = 2$ meets the line $y = 5$.

   (e) Write down the co-ordinates of the point where the line $x = 2$ meets the line $y = 2x + 2$.

In questions **1** to **6** you are given the coordinates of several points on a line. Find the equation of each line.

1

x	1	2	3	4	5
y	5	6	7	8	9

2

x	0	1	2	3	4
y	7	8	9	10	11

3

x	0	1	2	3
y	3	2	1	0

4

x	4	5	6	7	8
y	5	4	3	2	1

5

x	1	2	3	4	5
y	5	10	15	20	25

6

x	1	2	3	4	5
y	6	11	16	21	26

7 Find the equation of the line through
   (a) A and B
   (b) A and C
   (c) B and C

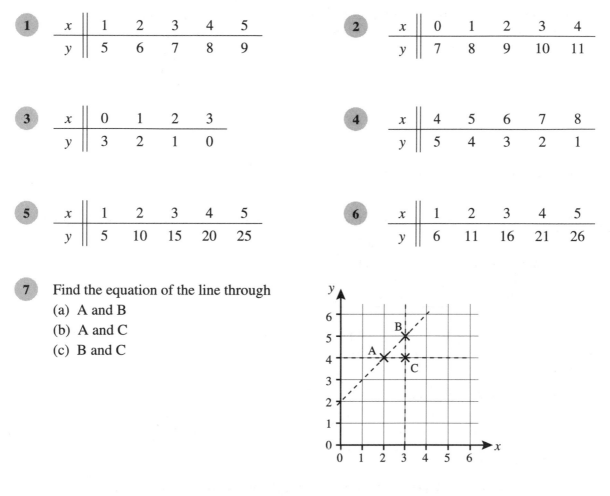

8

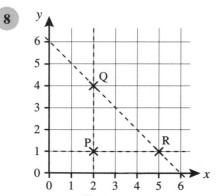

Find the equation of the line through
   (a) P and Q
   (b) P and R
   (c) Q and R

5.7 Area Review

1 Calculate the area of each shape. The lengths are in cm.

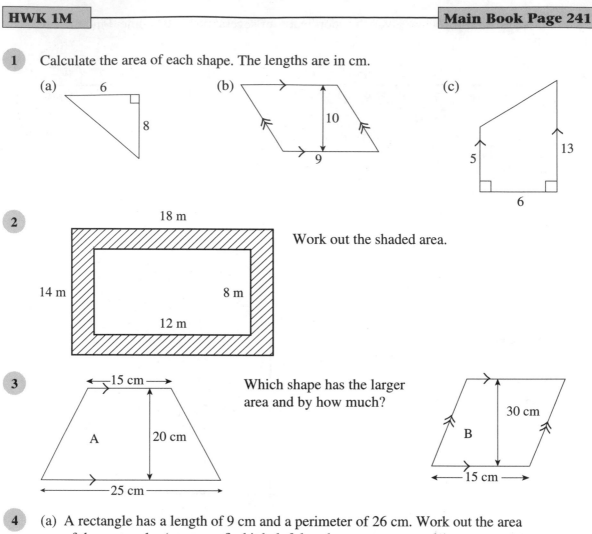

(a) 6, 8

(b) 10, 9

(c) 5, 13, 6

2 Work out the shaded area.

18 m, 14 m, 8 m, 12 m

3 Which shape has the larger area and by how much?

A: 15 cm, 20 cm, 25 cm

B: 30 cm, 15 cm

4 (a) A rectangle has a length of 9 cm and a perimeter of 26 cm. Work out the area of the rectangle. (you may find it helpful to draw out a rectangle)

(b) A square has the same area as the rectangle. Work out the perimeter of the square.

5 Find the value of x in each shape below.

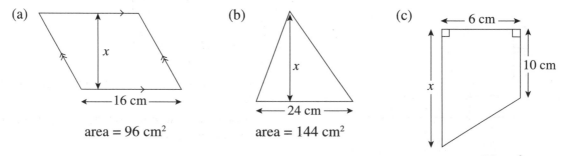

(a) x, 16 cm

area = 96 cm^2

(b) x, 24 cm

area = 144 cm^2

(c) 6 cm, 10 cm, x

area = 78 cm^2

HWK 1E ──────────────────────────── **Main Book Page 244**

1   Calculate the area of each circle and give your answer correct to one decimal place.

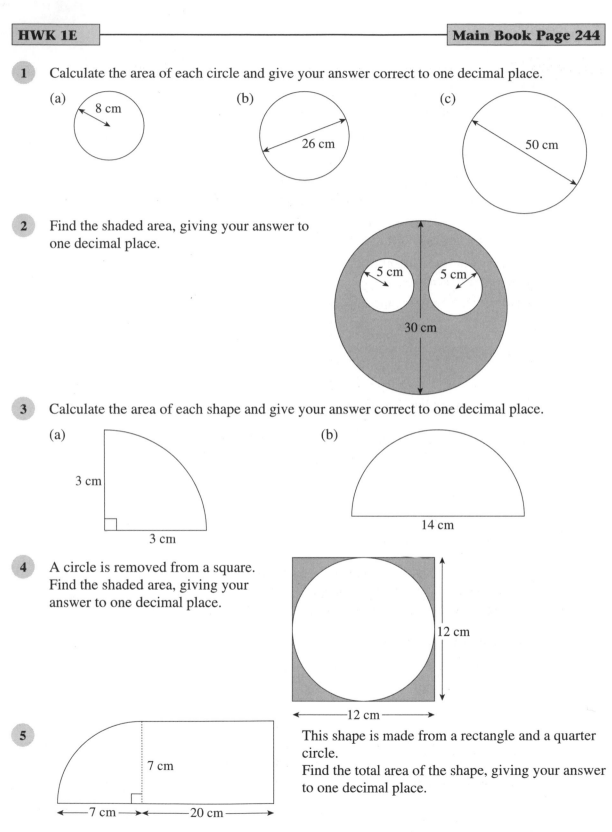

(a)   8 cm

(b)   26 cm

(c)   50 cm

2   Find the shaded area, giving your answer to one decimal place.

5 cm   5 cm

30 cm

3   Calculate the area of each shape and give your answer correct to one decimal place.

(a)   3 cm

3 cm

(b)   14 cm

4   A circle is removed from a square. Find the shaded area, giving your answer to one decimal place.

12 cm

12 cm

5   7 cm

7 cm — 20 cm

This shape is made from a rectangle and a quarter circle.
Find the total area of the shape, giving your answer to one decimal place.

UNIT 6

6.1 Percentages

HWK 1M ———————————————————— **Main Book Page 256**

1. 1000 people were asked if they were connected to the internet at home. 850 people said 'yes'. What percentage of the people said 'yes'?

2. Hatton United play 50 football games. They draw 9 games and lose 10 games. What percentage of the games did Hatton United win?

3. Over 200 days Martin is absent from school for 14 of them. For what percentage of the days did Martin come to school?

4. Four people obtain the test marks shown below.

Jane	Tobias	Hal	Meg
$\frac{11}{20}$	$\frac{20}{40}$	$\frac{108}{200}$	$\frac{13}{25}$

   (a) Change each mark into a percentage and write down each name in order of percentage, starting with the highest.
   (b) Meg scored a higher percentage than Tobias. How much more did she score?

5. Nina has to wash the evening dishes on four of the five weekdays. On what percentage of the weekdays does she *not* have to wash the evening dishes?

6. Matt has £60. He spends one third of his money on a shirt. He then sees a pair of trousers for £30. What percentage of his remaining money would he use if he buys the trousers?

7. Yasmin has 40 pairs of shoes. If 8 pairs of shoes are red, what percentage of her shoes are *not* red?

HWK 1E ———————————————————— **Main Book Page 257**

You may use a calculator. Give all answers to one decimal place.

1. 8 people out of 15 in a rugby team are more than 6 feet tall. What percentage of the team are more than 6 feet tall?

2.  What percentage of these faces are 'smiley'?

3 17 out of 163 people thought that 'Little Britain' was the best comedy programme ever. What percentage of the people was this?

4 A 150 g chocolate bar contains 59 g fat and 12 g fibre. What percentage of the chocolate bar is *not* fat or fibre?

5 The table shows how many children wear glasses in Year 8 at Denton High School.

(a) What percentage of the girls wear glasses?

(b) What percentage of all the children do not wear glasses?

	Boys	Girls	Total
wear glasses	17	28	45
do not wear glasses	74	102	176
Total	91	130	221

6 Three basketball players are shooting baskets. Their success rate is shown opposite.

(a) Who had the highest percentage rate of success?

(b) What was the percentage difference in success rates between Cheryl and Mike?

	successes	total attempts
Jason	39	143
Cheryl	48	170
Mike	27	71

7

	Men	Women	Total
under 21	174	263	437
21 to 65	320	419	739
over 65	211	306	517
Total	705	988	1693

One day a supermarket records the ages of the shoppers. This information is shown in the table.

(a) What percentage of the men were over 65?

(b) What percentage of the people were 21 to 65 years old?

(c) What percentage of the women were 65 or *under* 65 years old?

HWK 2M ——————————————————— **Main Book Page 258**

Do not use a calculator.

1 Answer true or false.

(a) 5% of £60 = £20   (b) 30% of £40 = £12   (c) 80% of £70 = £56

(d) 20% of £320 = £64   (e) 5% of £140 = £28   (f) 60% of £90 = £54

2 Neil has a house worth £340 000. Two years later its value has gone down by 20%. How much money has its value gone down by?

3 Find the odd one out

(a) 30% of £30   (b) 5% of £160   (c) 40% of £20

4 Which is larger?   3% of £600   or   4% of £500

5 Work out
(a) 2% of £5400   (b) 13% of £600   (c) 11% of £800

6 Work out
(a) 5% of £40   (b) $2\frac{1}{2}$% of £40   (c) $7\frac{1}{2}$% of £40

(d) $17\frac{1}{2}$% of £40   (e) $17\frac{1}{2}$% of £120   (f) $17\frac{1}{2}$% of £60

HWK 2E ———————————————————————— **Main Book Page 259**

You may use a calculator.

1 Work out

(a) 9% of £38   (b) 42% of £129   (c) 78% of £3200

2 There are 280 pupils in Year 11 in Mount Green High School.
55% of the pupils obtain a grade C or better in their GCSE Maths.

(a) How many pupils obtained a grade C or better in their GCSE Maths?

(b) How many pupils did not obtain a grade C or better?

3 Answer true or false.

(a) 16% of £92 = £15.72   (b) 8% of £27 = £2.16

4 John buys a house for £294 000. He has to pay a 2.5% tax called stamp duty.
How much tax does he pay?

5 A United Nations army unit is to be made up from soldiers from four nations as shown in the table.

(a) Write down how many soldiers are chosen from each country.

(b) From which country did the highest number of soldiers come from?

Country	Size of available force	Percentage chosen
UK	1600	3%
Germany	400	7%
Spain	250	12%
New Zealand	1400	2%

6 Remember: £15.1674 = £15.17 to the nearest penny. Write each amount below to the nearest penny.

(a) £23.2816   (b) £49.316   (c) £2.0774   (d) £138.5146

7 Work out, giving each answer correct to the nearest penny.

(a) 26% of £5.19   (b) 31% of £16.46

(c) 8.5% of £29.12   (d) 3.4% of £19.74

HWK 3M ───────────────────────────── **Main Book Page 261**

Do not use a calculator.

1. Marvin is trying to sell his car for £2500. He is not having much luck so decides to knock 20% off the selling price. How much is he asking for his car now?

2. (a) Decrease £240 by 5%. (b) Increase £80 by 15%.

3. The cost of a £560 TV is increased by 5%. What is the new cost of the TV?

4. A farmer keeps 60 pigs. During the next two years the number of pigs increases by 35%. How many pigs does the farmer now have?

5.
Amount A	Amount B
Reduce £2800 by 45%	Increase £1300 by 20%

   Which amount above is the larger and by how much?

6. Bianca has £640 in her bank account. She decides to use 85% of this money for a holiday. How much money is left in her bank account?

7.

   shirt £32 25% off   dress £45 40% off   skirt £30 20% off

   Naomi has £25. Which items above could she buy?

8. Mrs Oliver invests £5400 in a savings scheme. After 3 years her money has increased by 15%. How much money does she now have in the savings scheme?

HWK 3E ───────────────────────────── **Main Book Page 261**

You may use a calculator.

1. The cost of a £49 train ticket to London is increased by 4%. What is the new cost of the ticket?

2. (a) Increase £160 by 18%. (b) Decrease £65 by 9%.

3 Joe has £42 and spends 63% of his money. Beth has £73 and spends 78% of her money. Who has more money left and by how much?

4 Terry is building a garage and has used 350 bricks so far. He needs to use a further 82% of the bricks used so far. How many bricks will he use in total?

5

| radio £59 20% off | digital camera £314 15% off | cd player £93 30% off |

Hannah buys all 3 items above in the sale.
How much does she pay in total?

6 Molly's gas bill is £114 plus an extra 5% (known as Value Added Tax). How much does Molly have to pay in total?

7 Lucy's garage bill is £210 plus an extra 17.5% (known as Value Added Tax). How much does Lucy have to pay in total?

8

Last year
Cornet £1.80
Sales 1060

This year
Cornet price increased by 20%
Sales decrease by 20%

Each year Alfonso sells ice-creams at the Banwell festival.

(a) Did Alfonso make more money, the same money or less money on selling cornets this year compared to last year?

(b) Write down the difference in the amount of money he made.

6.2 Probability

HWK 1M ──────────────────────────── **Main Book Page 263**

1

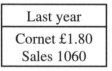

With this spinner find the probability of getting:

(a) a 5

(b) a multiple of 4

(c) a prime number

(d) not an even number

2 The probability of Sid's dog barking sometime in the morning is 0.97.
What is the probability of Sid's dog not barking sometime in the morning?

3 A dice is thrown. What is the probability of getting:

(a) a 3   (b) a number less than 5   (c) a square number

4

One card is chosen from above at random.

Find the probability of getting:

(a) an 'S'   (b) not a 'T'   (c) a vowel

5 47% at the children in Year 8 in Colne Community School are boys.
When Year 8 walk into an assembly, what is the probability that the first
child to arrive will be a girl?

6 A pack of cards has 13 clubs, 13 diamonds, 13 hearts and 13 spades.

One card is selected at random from the pack.

Find the probability of selecting:

(a) a heart   (b) not a club

7

$$\pi = 3 . 1 4 1 5 9 2 6$$

One digit is chosen at random from the digits shown above.

What is the probability of selecting:

(a) the digit '1'   (b) a digit which is not a prime number

HWK 1E ———————————————————— **Main Book Page 265**

1

Two bags have red (R)
and black (B) balls in
them as shown.

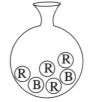

(a) Find the probability of selecting a black ball from bag A.

(b) A black ball is taken from bag A and put into bag B. A ball is then selected at random
from bag B. What is the probability that this ball is not a black ball?

2

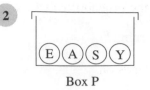

Box P

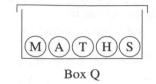

Box Q

Two boxes contain discs as shown.

(a) One disc is removed from box P. What is the probability of selecting a vowel? The disc is placed back in box P.

(b) Four more discs, **V** **E** **R** **Y** , are added to box P. If one disc is now removed from box P, what is the probability of selecting a vowel? The disc is placed back in box P.

(c) The disc **A** is now taken out of box Q and placed in box P. If one disc is now removed from box P, what is the probability of selecting a vowel?

3 (a) Colin has a box with Mars bars and Milky Way bars inside it. If a bar is taken at random from the box, the probability of picking a Mars bar is $\frac{5}{7}$.

What is the probability of picking a Milky Way?

(b) How many Mars Bars could there be in Colin's box to start with?

(c) Write down another two possibilities for the number of Mars bars that might be in Colin's box to start with.

4

S	U	R	E	W	A	Y

This old supermarket sign is in bad repair. One of the letters drops off.

(a) What is the probability that a vowel drops off.

(b) The letter 'E' drops off. If another letter drops off, what is the probability that it will be a vowel?

5 Will has the Jack, Queen, King, Ace of Clubs and the Ace of Hearts. Amy chooses one of his cards then Mark chooses one of his cards.

(a) If Amy chooses an Ace, what is the probability of Mark choosing an Ace?

(b) If Amy chooses a King, what is the probability of Mark choosing an Ace?

HWK 2E ──────────────────────────────────── **Main Book Page 267**

1 A bag contained some discs. Each disc has one of three letters on it – 'T', 'R', or 'Y'. Jan randomly takes a disc from the bag and then replaces it. She does this 80 times and records the results.

Letter	T	R	Y
Frequency	23	34	23

Use the results shown at the bottom of the previous page to estimate the probability that the next disc she takes out will be

(a) a 'Y'   (b) an 'R'

2 Lara rolls a fair dice 120 times. Each time she records the number it lands on.

Number	1	2	3	4	5	6
Frequency	22	25	4	23	27	19

(a) What seems 'strange' about these results?
(b) How many times would you have expected the dice to land on each different number?
(c) If Lara rolled the dice another 120 times, would you expect her to get the same results?

3 Chad and Marie throw a shoe to see if it will land on its heel or not. Chad throws 50 times and Marie throws 130 times. The results are shown below.

Chad
Throws	50
Heel landings	28

Marie
Throws	130
Heel landings	57

The shoe is thrown again.

(a) For Chad, what is the probability of the shoe landing on its heel?
(b) For Marie, what is the probability of the shoe landing on its heel?
(c) If you put Chad's and Marie's results together, what is the probability of the shoe landing on its heel if it is thrown again?

4 Toss a coin 50 times. How many tails would you expect to get?
Write down how your results compare to what you expected to get.

HWK 3M/3E   **Main Book Page 269**

1 (a) For lunch, Alana eats pizza or pasta and drinks coke or lemonade. Copy and complete the table below to show all the different lunches she might have.

Food	Drink
pizza	coke
pizza	

(b) What is the probability that Alana has pasta and coke for her lunch?

2 (a) A mother has 2 children. Copy and complete the table to show if each child is a boy or a girl.

1st child	2nd child
boy	boy

(b) What is the probability that a mother will have two girls?

3 (a) Ellie throws a coin and a dice. She could get a 'head' and a '5' (H 5). She could get a 'tail' and a '5' (T 5). List the 12 possible outcomes.

(b) What is the probability that Ellie would get a 'tail' and an odd number?

4 (a) Mindy uses a spinner (with the numbers 1, 2 and 3 on it) and a dice.

She could get a '2' with the spinner and a '4' with the dice (2, 4).

She could get a '2' with the spinner and a '5' with the dice (2, 5). List the 18 possible outcomes.

(b) What is the probability that she will get an odd number with both the spinner and the dice?

5 (a) 2 dice are thrown. List all possible outcomes (there are 36 ways!) Copy and complete:

$$
\begin{array}{cccccc}
(1, 1) & (2, 1) & (3, 1) & (4, 1) & (5, 1) & (6, 1) \\
(1, 2) & (2, 2) & (3, 2) & \ldots & \ldots & \ldots \\
(1, 3) & \ldots & \ldots & \ldots & \ldots & \ldots \\
\ldots & \ldots & \ldots & \ldots & \ldots & \ldots
\end{array}
$$

(b) What is the probability of throwing the same number on each dice?

6 A mother has 3 children. List all the possible outcomes to show if each child is a boy or a girl. What is the probability that all 3 children will be boys?

6.3 Measures

HWK 1M ———————————————— **Main Book Page 273**

Remember: 1 km = 1000 m   1 kg = 1000 g   1 litre = 1000 ml   and   1 tonne = 1000 kg.

Copy and complete the following:

1 7400 m = _____ km   **2** 40 mm = _____ cm   **3** 35 cm = _____ m

4 2.5 kg = _____ g   **5** 4500 ml = _____ litres   **6** 6.8 km = _____ m

7 320 g = _____ kg   **8** 6.5 tonnes = _____ kg   **9** 2.38 m = _____ cm

10 4.2 km = _____ m   **11** 3.4 litres = _____ ml   **12** 400 kg = _____ tonnes

13 Simon uses 450 g and 720 g of plain flour when baking. He started with 3 kg of plain flour. How much plain flour has he now got left?

14 Louise pours 740 ml of oil into her car engine from a 3 litre can. How many more times would she be able to pour 740 ml from this can of oil?

15 Which would be worth more?

| Six 165 kg bars of gold | or | One 1 tonne block of gold |

16 Henry earns 35p each minute. He works for 12 hours each day, five days a week. How much does he earn in one year? (take one year to be 50 weeks).

17 The total weight of 15 players in a rugby team is 1.6 tonnes. A 112 kg player leaves the field because of injury. What is the total weight of the remaining 14 players?

18 A glass of orange juice contains 85 ml. How many glasses can be filled from a 1.5 litre carton of orange juice?

HWK 1E ──────────────────────── **Main Book Page 274**

Converting between metric and imperial units

1 m ≈ 3 feet   1 kg ≈ 2.2 pounds

8 km ≈ 5 miles   1 gallon ≈ 4.5 litres

1 litre is just less than 2 pints

1 foot = 12 inches   1 yard = 3 feet

1 stone = 14 pounds   1 pound = 16 ounces

1 For each pair below, write down which is the larger amount.

(a) 24 km, 16 miles   (b) 5 feet, 59 inches

(c) 20 feet, 6 yards   (d) 3 kg, 7 pounds

(e) 5 gallons, 20 litres   (f) 12 pints, 4 litres

(g) 90 pounds, 7 stones   (h) 32 miles, 60 km

(i) 90 litres, 16 gallons   (j) 50 ounces, 4 pounds

2 Luke is 5 feet 6 inches tall and Gwen is 70 inches tall. What is the difference in their heights?

3 Sandeep puts 7 gallons of petrol into his car. He then uses 30 litres during his journey. How many litres of petrol remain from the 7 gallons?

4 Answer true or false.

(a) An 'average' man's foot is about 24 cm long.

(b) An 'average' young woman weighs about 126 pounds.

(c) A can of coke contains about 3 pints.

5 A man weighs 10 stone 3 pounds and a woman weighs 68 kg. Who is heavier and by how much?

108

6.4 Algebra Review

HWK 1M ──────────────────────────── **Main Book Page 276**

For questions **1** to **12** , use $a = 5$, $b = 2$ and $c = 9$ to find the value of each expression.

1 $3b$

2 ac

3 $5a - 4b$

4 $8c + 3a$

5 $\dfrac{4a}{b}$

6 c^2

7 $c^2 - a^2$

8 $4b + b^2$

9 $\dfrac{10b}{a}$

10 $c^2 - a^2 + b^2$

11 abc

12 $\dfrac{a^2 - c}{b}$

Collect the like terms in questions **13** to **16** .

13 $4m + 6n - 2n + 4m$

14 $3p + 5q + 6p - 2q$

15 $9a + 3b - 4a + 3$

16 $6 + 4x - 2x + 9 - x$

17   Tim has £y. He spends £w on a book and £5 on bus travel. Write down on expression for the money he now has left.

18
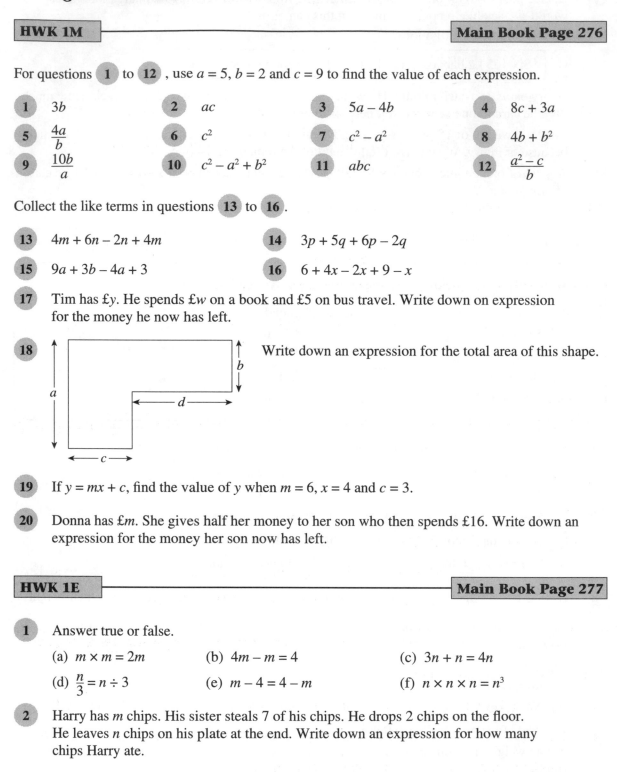
Write down an expression for the total area of this shape.

19   If $y = mx + c$, find the value of y when $m = 6$, $x = 4$ and $c = 3$.

20   Donna has £m. She gives half her money to her son who then spends £16. Write down an expression for the money her son now has left.

HWK 1E ──────────────────────────── **Main Book Page 277**

1   Answer true or false.

   (a) $m \times m = 2m$

   (b) $4m - m = 4$

   (c) $3n + n = 4n$

   (d) $\dfrac{n}{3} = n \div 3$

   (e) $m - 4 = 4 - m$

   (f) $n \times n \times n = n^3$

2   Harry has m chips. His sister steals 7 of his chips. He drops 2 chips on the floor. He leaves n chips on his plate at the end. Write down an expression for how many chips Harry ate.

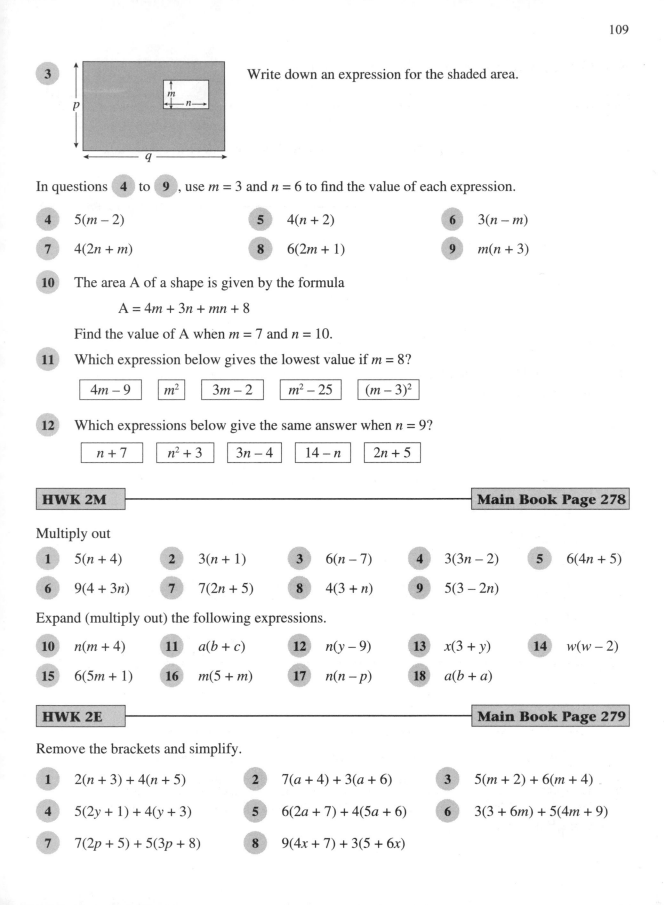

3 Write down an expression for the shaded area.

In questions **4** to **9**, use $m = 3$ and $n = 6$ to find the value of each expression.

4 $5(m - 2)$

5 $4(n + 2)$

6 $3(n - m)$

7 $4(2n + m)$

8 $6(2m + 1)$

9 $m(n + 3)$

10 The area A of a shape is given by the formula

$$A = 4m + 3n + mn + 8$$

Find the value of A when $m = 7$ and $n = 10$.

11 Which expression below gives the lowest value if $m = 8$?

| $4m - 9$ | m^2 | $3m - 2$ | $m^2 - 25$ | $(m - 3)^2$ |

12 Which expressions below give the same answer when $n = 9$?

| $n + 7$ | $n^2 + 3$ | $3n - 4$ | $14 - n$ | $2n + 5$ |

HWK 2M ———————————————————— **Main Book Page 278**

Multiply out

1 $5(n + 4)$　　**2** $3(n + 1)$　　**3** $6(n - 7)$　　**4** $3(3n - 2)$　　**5** $6(4n + 5)$

6 $9(4 + 3n)$　　**7** $7(2n + 5)$　　**8** $4(3 + n)$　　**9** $5(3 - 2n)$

Expand (multiply out) the following expressions.

10 $n(m + 4)$　　**11** $a(b + c)$　　**12** $n(y - 9)$　　**13** $x(3 + y)$　　**14** $w(w - 2)$

15 $6(5m + 1)$　　**16** $m(5 + m)$　　**17** $n(n - p)$　　**18** $a(b + a)$

HWK 2E ———————————————————— **Main Book Page 279**

Remove the brackets and simplify.

1 $2(n + 3) + 4(n + 5)$

2 $7(a + 4) + 3(a + 6)$

3 $5(m + 2) + 6(m + 4)$

4 $5(2y + 1) + 4(y + 3)$

5 $6(2a + 7) + 4(5a + 6)$

6 $3(3 + 6m) + 5(4m + 9)$

7 $7(2p + 5) + 5(3p + 8)$

8 $9(4x + 7) + 3(5 + 6x)$

110

Simplify these expressions by removing the brackets first.

9 $6(a + 4) + 3(a - 5)$

10 $4(m + 2) - 2(m - 3)$

11 $5(2n + 3) - 3(3n - 4)$

12 $4(2x + 7) - 3(2x + 3)$

13 $8(3y + 5) - 4(2y - 5)$

14 $7(3w + 4) - 5(2w + 5)$

15 $6(5n + 3) + 4(2n - 1)$

16 $9(7a + 4) - 8(5a - 2)$

HWK 3M ———————————————————————— **Main Book Page 280**

Solve the equations.

1 $n - 9 = 13$

2 $6n = 30$

3 $5n - 3 = 17$

4 $6n + 9 = 57$

5 $7 + 4n = 35$

6 $86 = 9n - 4$

7 $19 = 7n - 16$

8 $3n + 39 = 75$

9 $44 = 12 + 8n$

10 If I treble a number n and then subtract 14, the answer is 25. Write down an equation and solve it to find the value of n.

Solve these equations.

11 $4(n + 3) = 32$

12 $6(n - 5) = 42$

13 $5(n - 2) = 30$

14 $7(n - 1) = 70$

15 $56 = 8(n + 3)$

16 $27 = 3(2n + 1)$

17 $5(4 + n) = 45$

18 $3(3n - 2) = 30$

19 $110 = 10(3 + 4n)$

20 $\boxed{a + a + a + a = 24}$ $\boxed{b - a = 10}$ $\boxed{a + a + b + c = 36}$

Find the value of c.

HWK 3E ———————————————————————— **Main Book Page 281**

Solve the equations.

1 $6x + 7 = 3x + 25$

2 $8x - 6 = 6x + 2$

3 $5x - 16 = 2x + 14$

4 $4x + 27 = 2x + 45$

5 $5x + 45 = 9x - 15$

6 $7x + 33 = 54 + 4x$

7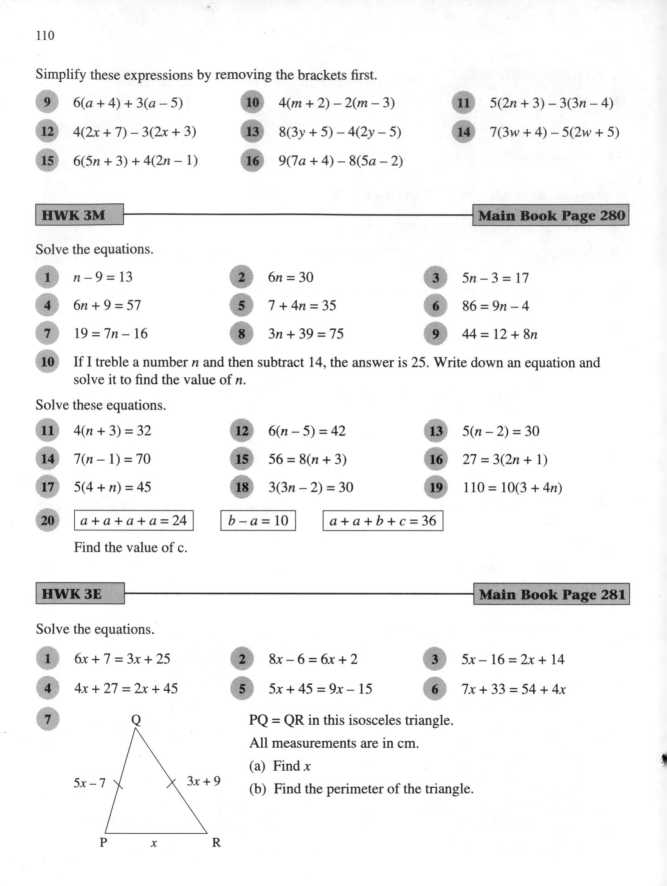

PQ = QR in this isosceles triangle.

All measurements are in cm.

(a) Find x

(b) Find the perimeter of the triangle.

Now solve these equations.

8 $5(x + 3) = 2(2x + 11)$ **9** $7(x + 6) = 11(2x - 3)$ **10** $4(2x - 3) = 3(2 + 2x)$

11 $3(4x + 1) = 9(2x - 1)$ **12** $8(2x - 7) = 2x$ **13** $6(x + 9) = 3(8 + 3x)$

14 $3(3x + 5) = 29(x - 5)$ **15** $10(9 + 2x) = 33(x - 2)$

6.5 3–D Objects

HWK 2M — **Main Book Page 286**

In questions **1** to **4** draw the plan view, the front view and the side view of the object.

1 plan view
side view
front view

2

3

4

In questions **5** to **8** you are given three views of a shape. Draw each 3–D object (like those shown above).

5
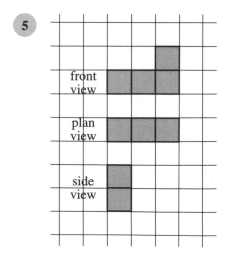
front view
plan view
side view

6
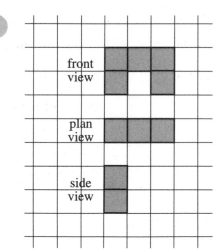
front view
plan view
side view

7

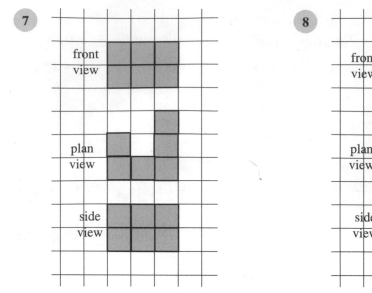

8

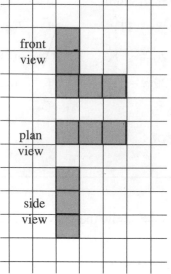

6.6 Bearings and scale drawing

HWK 1M ─────────────────────────────────── **Main Book Page 288**

1   Ten policemen are searching for a stolen car.
They all set off in different directions as shown.
On what bearing does each policeman travel?

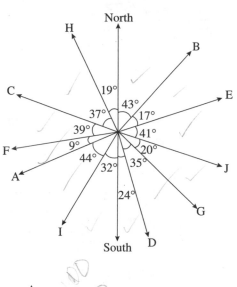

2   (a)   Write down the bearing of B from A.

(b)   Write down the bearing of A from B.

3

North

Q

115°)160°

85°

North

65°

255° 40°

P

North

20°

55°

R)285°

Write down the bearing of:

(a) Q from P

(b) R from Q

(c) R from P

(d) P from R

HWK 1E ——————————————————— **Main Book Page 288**

1 Measure the bearing of (a) A to B (b) C to D (c) E to F (d) G to H

(e) I to J (f) K to L (g) M to N

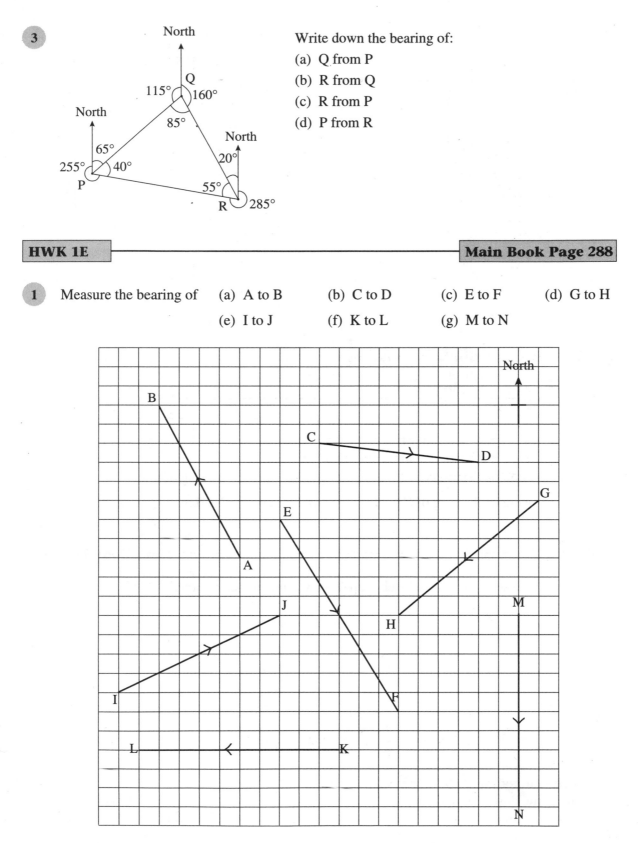

2 Draw lines to show the following bearings.

(a) 065°   (b) 170°   (c) 250°   (d) 155°   (e) 310°

3 A ship sails from A to P then to B. Another ship sails from C to Q then to D.

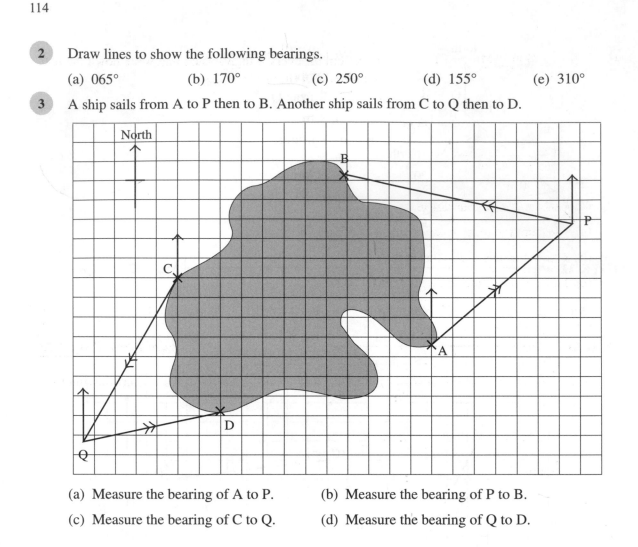

(a) Measure the bearing of A to P.   (b) Measure the bearing of P to B.

(c) Measure the bearing of C to Q.   (d) Measure the bearing of Q to D.

HWK 2M ———————————————————————— **Main Book Page 290**

Draw an accurate scale drawing of each shape below using the scale shown.

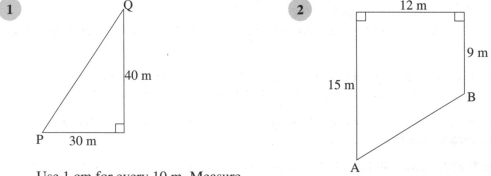

1

Q

40 m

P   30 m

Use 1 cm for every 10 m. Measure and write down the real length of PQ (in metres).

2

12 m

9 m

15 m

B

A

Use 1 cm for every 3 m. Measure and write down the real length of AB (in metres).

115

3 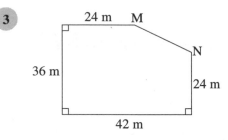 Use 1 cm for every 6 m. Measure and write down the real length of MN (in metres).

4 Choose a room in your house.

(a) Measure the longest length and write it down.

(b) Choose a sensible scale and write it down.

(c) Draw an accurate scale drawing of the room.

HWK 2E ──────────────────────────── **Main Book Page 292**

In questions **1** to **6** use a scale of 1 cm to represent 1 km. Draw an accurate scale drawing to help you answer each question.

1 A ship sails 7 km due north and then a further 5 km on a bearing 075°. How far is the ship now from its starting point?

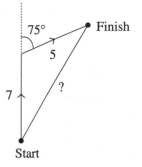

2 A ship sails 6 km due north and then a further 6 km on a bearing 080°. How far is the ship now from its starting point?

3 A man walks 8 km due west and then a further 5 km due south. How far is the man now from his starting point?

4 Sarah and Barclay are standing at the same point A. Sarah walks for 7 km on a bearing of 050°. Barclay walks for 6 km on a bearing of 310°. How far is Sarah from Barclay now?

5 A ship sails due south for 6 km then on a bearing of 120° for 3 km. How far is the ship now from its starting point?

6 Draw a point P with a cross. Point Q is 7 km from P on a bearing of 072° from P. Point R is 5 km from P on a bearing of 190° from P. What is the bearing of R from Q?

6.7 Decimals Review

Do not use a calculator.

1 Answer true or false.

(a) $7.42 + 3 = 7.45$ (b) $14 - 6.8 = 7.2$ (c) $8.1 + 6.49 + 3 = 17.59$

(d) $16.2 - 3.85 = 22.3$

2 The heights of five children are shown below:

Bryony	Cameron	Kelly	Sarwan	Lucy
165.3 cm	165.25 cm	165.31 cm	165.2 cm	165.09 cm

Write down the names in order of height, starting with the tallest.

3 What is 0.01 less than 2.3?

4 Which calculation gives a different answer to the other two?

| $16.5 + 9.38$ | | $31.4 - 8.18$ | | $33 - 7.12$ |

5 Write the number half way between 4.1 and 4.2

6 Write the number half way between 3.67 and 3.68

7 Write down the largest number shown below.

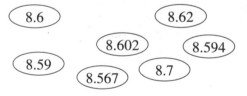

8.6   8.62   8.602   8.594   8.59   8.567   8.7

8 Write down the second largest number from the list of numbers in question **7** .

Do not use a calculator.

1 Answer true or false.

(a) $0.9 \times 0.03 = 0.27$ (b) $0.6^2 = 3.6$ (c) $16 \div 0.5 = 8$ (d) $0.268 \div 0.04 = 6.7$

2 How many 0.1 litre glasses of orange juice can be poured from a one litre carton?

3 Copy and complete this number chain.

$$0.07 \xrightarrow{\times 0.8} \boxed{} \xrightarrow{\div 0.02} \boxed{} \xrightarrow{\div 0.2} \boxed{}$$

4 Cinema tickets cost £7.45. How much will 14 tickets cost?

5 Work out

(a) 0.07×0.03 (b) $3.84 \div 0.8$ (c) 2.4×1.3

6 Some sweets cost £4.65 per kilogram. How much will 0.4 kg of sweets cost?

7 Copy and complete:

(a) $0.7 \times \boxed{} = 1.12$ (b) $\boxed{} \div 0.09 = 3.6$

8

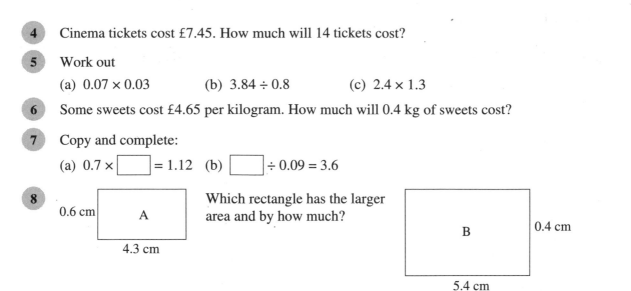

0.6 cm | A | 4.3 cm

Which rectangle has the larger area and by how much?

B | 0.4 cm | 5.4 cm

6.8 Volume

HWK 1M | **Main Book Page 297**

1 Write down the volume of each object. All the objects are made from centimetre cubes.

(a)

(b)

(c)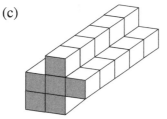

(d)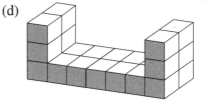

2 Work out the volume of each cuboid. Give your answer in the correct units.

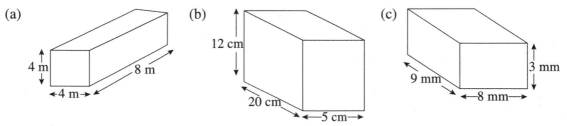

(a) 4 m, 4 m, 8 m (b) 12 cm, 20 cm, 5 cm (c) 9 mm, 8 mm, 3 mm

118

3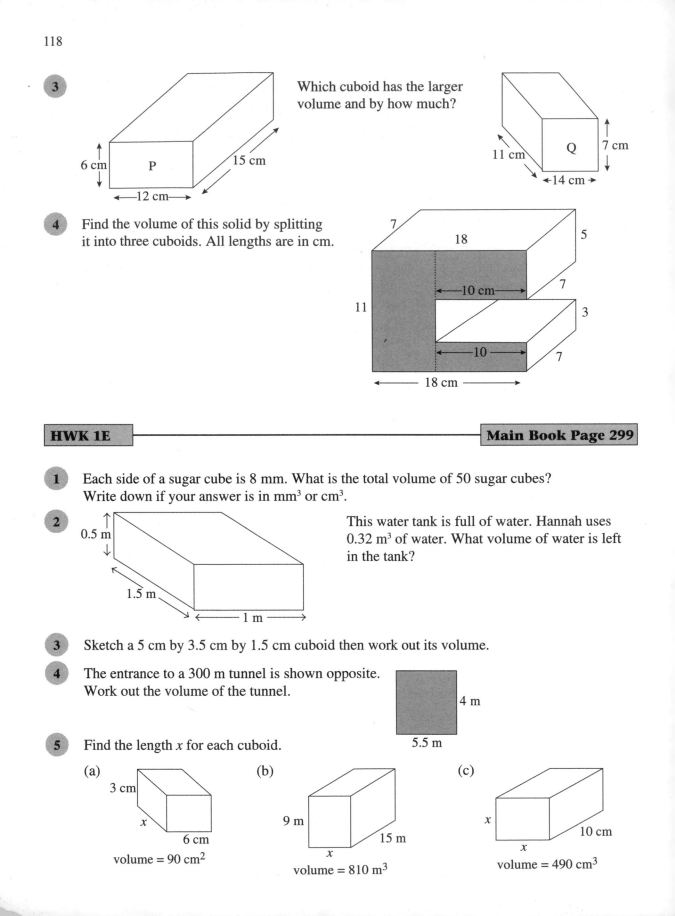

Which cuboid has the larger volume and by how much?

6 cm   P   15 cm   —12 cm—

11 cm   Q   7 cm   ←14 cm→

4 Find the volume of this solid by splitting it into three cuboids. All lengths are in cm.

7   18   5   7   ←10 cm→   11   3   ←10→   7   ← 18 cm →

HWK 1E ———————————————————— **Main Book Page 299**

1 Each side of a sugar cube is 8 mm. What is the total volume of 50 sugar cubes? Write down if your answer is in mm³ or cm³.

2 0.5 m   1.5 m   1 m

This water tank is full of water. Hannah uses 0.32 m³ of water. What volume of water is left in the tank?

3 Sketch a 5 cm by 3.5 cm by 1.5 cm cuboid then work out its volume.

4 The entrance to a 300 m tunnel is shown opposite. Work out the volume of the tunnel.

4 m   5.5 m

5 Find the length x for each cuboid.

(a) 3 cm x 6 cm   volume = 90 cm²

(b) 9 m x 15 m   volume = 810 m³

(c) x 10 cm x volume = 490 cm³

6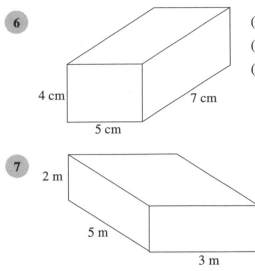

(a) Draw a *net* for this cuboid.

(b) Work out the volume of this cuboid.

(c) Work out the total surface area of this cuboid.

4 cm   7 cm

5 cm

7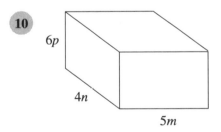

2 m

5 m

3 m

The container on a lorry is shown opposite. Sand is tipped into the lorry at a rate of 0.2 m³ per minute. How long does it take to completely fill the container with sand?

8 How many small cubes of side 0.1 m will fit into a large cube of side 2.4 m?

9 Write down an expression for the volume of this cuboid.

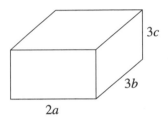

3c

3b

2a

10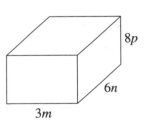

6p

4n

5m

Write down an expression for the difference in the volumes of these two cuboids.

8p

6n

3m